CW01024796

NATIONAL SERVICE 1950s
is an affectionate account by a graduate National Service conscript of how his life changed, in common with the lives of many tens of thousands of young men in the period after World War II, when he had to undergo the tough military basic training at Fulwood Barracks, Preston, further training at Wilton Park, Beaconsfield, and an extraordinary metamorphosis from trained to trainer in Tripoli and Homs during the benign rule of King Idris of Libya.

Told with humour and insight, John Kelly's story is at once deeply personal and yet instantly recognisable by men and their families suffering upheaval and recognising the benefits of growing up in a new world of foreign travel, absorbing sights, sounds and cultural differences.

With maps, illustrations, and a tribute to National Servicemen by John Kelly's former Commanding Officer at Homs, Brigadier (Retd.) P.A.L. Vaux, O.B.E.

* * *

John Kelly, after enjoying teaching in Libya during his National Service, decided to pursue a career in education. He completed postgraduate teacher-training in Cardiff, and taught history in comprehensive schools in South Wales. In 1997 he retired as head of the humanities faculty at Bassaleg Comprehensive School, Newport, and has since devoted his time to research and writing about National Service in Lancashire, Buckinghamshire and Libya. He has chosen not to return to Libya but to remember it as it was in the 1950s.

NATIONAL SERVICE 1950s

Lancs, Bucks, Libya

›››

JOHN KELLY

The Oleander Press

The Oleander Press
16 Orchard Street
Cambridge CB1 1JT

A CIP catalogue record for this book is available from the British Library.

ISBN 0 906672 34 1

Cover design by Peter Ducker
Maps by András Bereznay

Typeset in Great Britain and printed and bound in India.

Contents

List of Illustrations

* * *

Acknowledgements

My thanks are due to Philip Ward of The Oleander Press for patiently guiding me away from countless pitfalls. I must thank my sister Pat Elliott, and also Margaret Clode and Fay Ball for their constant encouragement. I am very grateful too to my old friend David Butler for many suggestions and much positive comment. An old national service friend, Lawrence Laidlaw, gave much help in recalling details, as did a number of former 6RTR officers: Peter Weaving, Martin Timmis and Keith Marr. Lieutenant Colonel (Retired) K.R. Bryan of the RAEC Association gave help too. Most of all I owe a debt of gratitude to Brigadier (Retired) Peter Vaux O.B.E., my former CO at 6RTR. He has constantly encouraged me, jogging my memory and helping me more than I can say. Any weaknesses or inaccuracies that might have crept into the text remain entirely my fault.

For permission to use photographs, I am grateful to the Museum of the Queen's Lancashire Regiment, Fulwood Barracks, Preston; Museum of The Royal Green Jackets; RAEC Association for Wilton Park Camp; Adjutant General's Corps Museum, Peninsular Barracks, Wiltshire; Centre for Buckinghamshire Studies for the picture of Beaconsfield; Jean Vaux; and Philip Ward. Others were taken by Alan Goodson, J.G. McEwan, Clive Canton and other old comrades. I have been unable to contact them but I trust they will be happy that I have made use of their photographs to enhance my narrative.

* * *

Foreword

Brigadier P.A.L. Vaux O.B.E.

The general public today scarcely remembers that in the critical post-war years of the 1950s and early 1960s the safety of our country, the keeping of the peace in our dwindling Empire and the defence of the ramparts at the Iron Curtain largely depended upon the involuntary service of our nation's male teenagers. A considerable Army by today's standards, largely composed of National Service conscripts between 18 and 20 years of age, served in such places as Hong Kong, Korea, Malaya, Kenya, North Africa and even the infamous Suez Operation of 1956. In Germany they faced a massive and threatening coalition of Soviet Armed Forces.

After many years' acquaintance with these young men, I had the great privilege of commanding two Royal Tank Regiments containing a great many of them. It was a special responsibility, too, for I knew from their parents' letters that I was held directly responsible for the wellbeing and safety of their children. One of these Regiments was located in Homs, 75 miles from Tripoli in Libya, at the request of King Idris, nervous of President Nasser in Egypt who felt jealous of Libya's potential oil wealth. With that inspired insensitivity which British Governments sometimes evince, they had selected for the task the 6th Royal Tank Regiment, which had spearheaded the attack on the Suez Canal. As it turned out, no harm seemed to have been done and the subject never arose. It was at Homs, around Christmas 1958, that John Kelly and I first met.

Much of the burden of training these young men fell upon a splendid hard core of Warrant Officers and Sergeants of great experience and integrity. But with these we had a particular problem. Many of these senior regulars, especially with wartime service, lacked the educational standard for advancement in an increasingly technical and sophisticated modern Army. It was painful to witness a competent and valuable NCO struggling to achieve a Certificate of Education upon which his professional future depended. Among the conscripts were of course university graduates, three or four years older than the others. Some of these became officers or were trained as technicians but the brilliant idea was conceived of selecting, from among those who had survived the arduous infantry basic training and were of an academic nature, those who might be trained as educational instructors at the Army School of Education at Beaconsfield in the rank of Sergeant and posted to units such as ours where they were badly needed. Here they performed invaluable work and many went on to distinguished teaching careers in both state and independent sectors.

Such a man was John Kelly. He was greatly welcome, especially to help our senior ranks among whom, by his sensitive courtesy, he soon settled comfortably and who readily accepted his instruction. Similarly, by being only a few years older than them, he gave many young national servicemen a lift into civilian life or qualified them to sign on as regulars. Several of our young officers sought help from the two Education NCOs and even my prep-school son was coached with his maths in the holidays. These men were, however, no mere 'schoolies', for they could handle rifle, machine-gun or Brasso as well as anyone and took their full part in regimental duties.

John Kelly has written a brilliantly readable and human account of his National Service, from the day he joined until his eventual demob – and the mixed feelings which accompanied that. I can vouch for the honesty, accuracy and lack of prejudice with which this narrative is written. It gives a welcome and fascinating insight into an almost forgotten period of British history.

For myself, I grew to love my often maddening but usually endearing young soldiers who arrived as adolescents and departed as well-trained, fit and mature adults. My wife and I have returned to Libya three times in the last four years, lastly in May 2001. We have been welcomed everywhere, especially in Homs, people saying 'British soldiers are always welcome here, for we do not forget that you rid us of the hated Italian colonial regime and stayed put to put us on our feet afterwards.' It has been said that the best ambassadors for Britain are her ordinary soldiers. Our National Servicemen played their full part in that rôle.

Prologue

One of the most abiding and vivid memories of my national service came right at its end. The troopship *Dunera* had docked at Southampton on a lovely summer's day in September 1959 and we had all disembarked. In what seemed no time at all we had arrived at the railway station. We said goodbyes in 1950s fashion, nothing too demonstrative, a pat on the shoulder here, a handshake there and soon, the 6th Royal Tanks had boarded their train, bound for their UK depôt in Dorset. I stood alone on the platform, kitbag at my side. As the train carrying my comrades moved off, a couple of troopers stuck their heads out of a window and waved. I lifted my hand and slowly waved back. Then the train rounded a bend and the 6th Royal Tanks moved out of my sight, and out of my life.

I moved on to another platform to catch a train to my own depôt, and demob. Thoughts crowded into my mind as I stood there alone. I remembered arriving alone on that very first day, dreading the thought of stepping out into the unknown. Now after two long but fascinating and educative years I stood alone again. And I felt, just for a moment, quite sad.

* * *

Army Book 111

A 080836

REGULAR ARMY

CERTIFICATE
OF
NATIONAL SERVICE

Any person finding this book is requested to hand it in to any Barracks, Post Office or Police Station, for transmission to the Under-Secretary of State, The War Office, London, S.W.1

1

Civilian life already seemed far away

I left the train at Preston, carrying the few belongings I had been told to bring with me: toothbrush, toothpaste, razor, and looked around the platform wondering where I was supposed to go next. A few seconds later I caught sight of a large sign which read, 'East Lancashire Regiment' and observed a couple of exceedingly well turned out soldiers, one a corporal, the other a lance corporal. One or two young men in civilian clothes stood nearby looking as if they might have been waiting a while. Others from my train began to gather round. It would be a long time before I again wondered what I had to do or where I had to go. I did not quite know it then but the Army was about to take over my life. The date was 12 September 1957.

'Over here; come on then; look sharp; haven't got all day. Anyone else? Line up! That's right. Truck's outside. Get a move on. This way.'

The voices sounded pleasantly North Lancashire in tone and, though brisk, not unfriendly. They bundled us into a three-ton truck and closed up the back tightly so we saw absolutely nothing of Preston on that first day. Indeed we saw nothing at all of Preston for some time to come. After about fifteen minutes the truck halted and we heard voices in the distance. The truck moved on a few yards, then halted again and they opened the back.

'Come on; out you get; line up; no, not like that; stand there; you behind; that's right; stand still!' We had arrived at Fulwood Barracks.

An enormous parade ground, the square, stretched ahead of us, and in the distance soldiers marched here and there to shouts of 'right whee-el,' and 'le-e-eft turn.' At the side, looking after the gate, stood two members of the regimental police, in very smart BD (battledress) and white webbing. The square was surrounded on all sides by what looked like stone-built terraced housing with Georgian sash windows but were in fact barrack rooms, one of

Fulwood Barracks. Entrance in the 1950s.

which soon became our new home. To the left of the gate, on the far left side of the square, stood the barrack blocks of the East Lancashire Regiment; we learned later that the barrack blocks to the far right, facing the East Lancashires, belonged to some 'inferior' people called The Loyals (Loyal Regiment, North Lancashire). I glanced at the outer wall of the barracks some fifteen feet high. I had never been inside a prison but I remember thinking at that moment that prison must look and feel something like this.

We marched along the perimeter towards the left till we reached a barrack block about halfway along the length of the left side of the square. As we stood outside, they called names, allocated numbers and explained things. 'Answer, yes, corporal,' came the order.

They divided us into four groups, two upstairs, and two downstairs. Corporal Bowerbank took charge of the downstairs groups. The lance corporal, under Corporal Bowerbank's direction, took charge of the upstairs groups. We entered the large front door into a wide passage which ran the width of the building to another door at the back. To the right and left I noticed the ground floor rooms. Lance Corporal Cottam led his groups up the stone staircase on the left. At a half landing it turned on itself and continued upwards. At the top other rooms exactly mirrored the ones below and the ten of us in my group entered the barrack room on the left. A huge fireplace and a large bunker of coal faced the doorway. On either side of the fireplace stood army-type metal beds, three to each side. More beds flanked each side of the door, every bed having a tall locker next to it. To the far right we could see Lance Corporal Cottam's bed and locker. Unlike the other beds, its grey blankets, sheets and pillows lay at the top end, very neatly folded and squared off and on the top of his locker I noticed some pristine and gleaming webbing and equipment that we soon learned to call top-kit. At each end of the room were two large windows. The wooden floorboards had been well polished. We each took a bed more or less at random.

The lance corporal said very little at this stage. He was young, perhaps 19, a slim, slight figure of medium height, impeccably turned out in BD. He appeared rather tense. One stripe, or tape as they called it, adorned each arm; this tape, we later realised, gave him absolute power over us recruits.

We had hardly had a chance to look round before the voice of Corporal Bowerbank called us down, and we fell in on the roadway outside the barrack block. The corporal informed us that we were going to 'the stores to get you all fixed up so that you can start looking like soldiers.' He had a rich Lancashire voice with a touch of exasperated humour in it. He immediately gave the impression of being a bit of a character, and a decent one at that; someone we could trust and talk to; someone who would help us when we needed it. Impeccably turned out, he looked every inch a confident and highly competent soldier. According to a rumour, both NCOs were national servicemen who had done so well in training that they had been selected to train others. Lance Corporal Cottam was newly made up, hence his slight air of nervous tension. Corporal Bowerbank somehow gave the impression that he had been in the Army for years; in fact it must have been less than two!

At the stores they doled us out a massive amount of kit, everything we would need: two sets of BD, gloves, dark green jersey, two pairs of boots, three pairs of thick light grey army socks, green drawers cellular (boxer shorts with a drawer string at the top), green vests, pyjamas, beret, cap badge, greatcoat, groundsheet (worn as a cape in the rain), PT shorts, gym shoes, two sets of denims (trousers and tops), braces, housewife (small bundle of needles and thread for the use of), towels, pint mug, knife, fork, and spoon, mess tins, webbing belt, and a mass of other webbing (haversacks, water-bottle etc.). We signed for the lot and made our way back to our new home, the barrack room, and dumped everything on the bed.

Seconds later, at about 5.30 pm, still dressed in civvies, we marched down to the cookhouse for our evening meal, mug, knife, fork, spoon held behind our backs in the right hand. As we entered the large square dining-room full of denim clad young recruits, they let out a huge roar of welcome. It sounded just a tiny bit derisory of course because we were now the new and rawest recruits, but it was a real welcome nevertheless from people in the same boat as us. It brought a smile to all our faces, and somehow we began to feel just little bit better. It crossed my mind that, in about three weeks time, we would be sitting down there cheering the next new intake: how I looked forward to that! We queued up to receive our food from the ACC (Army Catering Corps) cooks who wielded huge ladles and dished cottage pie and potatoes and vegetables on our plates. We each helped ourselves to a mug full of tea from a huge urn despite the fact that one denim clad youth shouted out that it was full of bromide.

The ten of us from our upstairs room sat together and began for the first time to talk to each other and we made the first beginnings in welding together what would become an incredibly close community. The faces around me, and mine too I suppose, must have looked strained. No one put on an act of bravado: the situation was too serious for that! As we ate our meal we spoke honestly about our concerns and fears. I think we all realised that we needed to admit our vulnerability to each other and to ourselves and just help each other through it all. Afterwards we cleaned our utensils and mugs in a huge vat of near boiling water, then placed them in another to rinse them. We walked slowly back to the barrack room.

We found the ablutions and made use of them: lavatories, wash basins, baths, all of them Victorian in appearance but of course, this being the Army, incredibly clean. The ablutions lay behind the barrack block, just through the back door and across another roadway.

The lance corporal stood waiting for us in the barrack room. He had put a match to the large fire in the huge fireplace, and it had already crackled into life.

'Right,' he said, 'off with those civvies, you won't need them for a long while; we'll send them home for you. Put your denims on.'

We changed into army underwear, and denims and the rest, an important moment that seemed to propel us truly and irrevocably into the forces. We rolled up every item of civilian clothing, and placed them neatly at the bottom of the locker as instructed. The boots proved hideously uncomfortable: no one knew then that after a week or so, when they had adapted to our feet, they would be the most comfortable footwear we had ever worn. The gaiters – anklets that fitted over the tops of the boots and into which we tucked our denim trousers – I put on with some difficulty and pulled tight with the two leather straps attached to them. I found the army shirt a bit prickly. They told us how to tie the tie: 'no windsor knots!' They told us that the beret must be shrunk, and how to fit the cap badge, and of course how to wear the beret: 'Rim one inch over the left eye, like this, and absolutely horizontal all the way round the back: got that?' I do not know what I looked like at that moment, but the other nine in the barrack room were beginning to look remarkably like those quite military looking recruits that we had seen in the cookhouse.

Top-kit, a complex of webbing, and small and large packs, water-bottle and so on we placed on top of our tall lockers.

'You will need to work on that lot till it looks like mine,' he said, nodding towards the gleaming, squared off, green blancoed arrangement on top of his locker.

'See these brasses?' He pointed to the brasses on his belt, and the buttons on his immaculate BD. 'And these?' He pointed to a multitude of brasses on his top-kit. 'And your cap badge? They must be polished every night with Brasso till they're perfect for inspection and that believe me will keep you busy. Concentrate first on those cap badges. Being at eye level they'll be noticed more than most things I can tell you.' The East Lancashire Regiment cap badge was a handsome one with the sphinx of Egypt engraved upon it along with the words EGYPT and EAST LANCASHIRE.

I think we all felt more than a bit dismayed by this time, and trapped. These people had total control over us, and this would be going on for two whole years! The only cheerful thing at that point was the fire, a mass of flames shooting up the chimney, making the barrack room begin to look and feel warm, cosy and almost homely.

At that point Corporal Bowerbank burst in followed by the groups from the other rooms. Suddenly things felt better!

'Right lads,' he said in his booming voice, 'it's not so bad is it? Some of you even look like soldiers already! Now to help cheer you up, I'm going to tell you how to bull up your boots, so that they're a credit to the best regiment in the British Army, the East Lancashires, and don't let me hear anybody calling them the East Lancs! We're the East Lancashires. And be proud of that cap badge. See that sphinx? That marks a battle won a long time ago in Egypt. When you're trained soldiers you'll get to wear this,' and he pointed to a diamond-shaped primrose yellow flash that both he and Lance Corporal Cottam wore behind their cap badges. 'Now, your boots, the soldier's best friend.' He pointed to the man next to him: 'Give me your best boots – no, not the ones you're wearing – your best boots!'

The corporal had a natural but friendly and positive authority which we came to admire greatly in time, though not at first, it has to be said. He could well have been younger than we because everyone in our particular barrack room was a graduate who had had his service deferred till the age of 21, but he looked the master here, and totally confident. In the presence of the master, the lance corporal too began to relax a little. Corporal Bowerbank shoved a spoon into the fire. When it glowed red hot, he applied it to the boot.

'All these pimples must be burned off but don't overdo it.' Smoke and the smell of burnt leather filled the room. 'Now, with a bit of water in the lid of your Kiwi black boot polish tin, and a duster, and round circular movements like this, you'll soon have boots that you can see your face in. OK, you can get on with that tomorrow night. Now, go down for an hour at the NAAFI (Navy Army and Air Force Institutes). And get yourselves some blanco, a blanco brush, two dusters, some Kiwi black boot polish, and a tin of Brasso. Anyone got no money? If so, borrow some till pay-day. Get back here by 9.30. You've an early start tomorrow.'

We trudged down to the NAAFI, which we had noticed on the way back from the cookhouse, full of talk about the iniquities of life and how unfair it all was, and how on earth would we ever survive, and so on.

As we approached the building that housed the NAAFI, we heard, emerging from the juke-box, the strains of Paul Anka's *Diana*. It was easily the most popular song at Fulwood in those days of basic training, and we were to hear its strains over and over again, till we knew every word by heart.

When the juke-box was not playing *Diana*, it was usually playing Elvis Presley singing *I'm all shook up*, a song that seemed more and more in keeping with how we felt, as the training at Fulwood proceeded. It certainly proved a popular hit with one lad in the barrack room. He admitted to being a big Elvis fan.

We found the NAAFI warm and friendly, full of young recruits who in the main seemed to be eating 'chips with everything'. We had no army food after the evening meal at about 5 o'clock. We drank cups of tea and began to talk to each other, hesitantly at first and then with increasing fervour. Dave Brown from Glasgow expressed reasoned outrage, suggesting we should not tolerate such treatment. Others agreed. Most of us though just felt resigned to it all and a lot of joking about boot burning took place. 'And why on earth should we have to bull up all that ridiculous webbing?' asked one Yorkshire lad. Another Dave, Dave Jeeves from Croft near Darlington, a bit of a character with a quizzical sense of humour, and someone who undoubtedly would become the leader of our group, told us we'd all just have to get on with it and make the best of it, and stick together and help each other out. We had no choice. We had to survive somehow. He later referred to himself as a B.A. (failed) from Hull University, but we recognised him as the brightest person in our group. We all thought that Corporal Bowerbank seemed not too bad.

At 9.30 we returned and went straight to bed by 10.00. Lance Corporal Cottam switched out the lights. The bed felt surprisingly comfortable and warm, and the room blissfully silent; a warm glow from the fire cast shadows as I fell asleep after my first day in the Army.

* * *

When I awoke, the fire had long since died down and I lay still in the darkness and silence. I knew they blew reveille at 6.00 a.m. but my hope that there might be time to lie there in the warmth before the bugle sounded proved fleeting indeed. I heard that unmistakable call, a bit distant but dauntingly military in tone. Seconds later all the lights were switched full on, and both corporals appeared, transformed into a frenzy, striding up and down the room, banging on the iron bed ends.

'Wakey wakey; rise and shine; up you get you lot. Get out of those beds you lazy sods. Time for kip is over. Now move it! Move yourselves.'

As one we sprang out of bed, and began feverishly the quite complicated process of getting dressed, boots and gaiters being the most difficult things for our inexperienced fingers to manage quickly. The corporal shouted his orders as we pulled on our clothes.

'Never mind those shirts, leave them there. Down you go; get washed and shaved and get back quick. These beds have to be made up, and we march to breakfast at 6.30.'

We rushed down the stairs and out to the back, washed in piping hot water then, ablutions completed, we raced back up.

The lance corporal now gave essential instructions on making up the beds. They had to be stripped of their white sheets and grey army blankets. We laid the bed cover over the mattress. Sheets and blankets had to be folded very neatly to the size of the pillows, two sheets in the centre and two blankets on the outside, and then another blanket had to be wrapped in a neat square around the whole thing. Pillows had to be put in position. He pointed to his bed in the corner, perfectly made up.

None of us achieved perfection on that first occasion but some whose efforts were pathetically inadequate had to do it again until they became fairly acceptable. As the weeks went by we became adept at achieving perfection quickly.

'Now get those berets on. Remember, cap badge one inch over the left eye, and make sure that the rim is horizontal all the way round!'

He inspected each one, and pulled and tugged at several before being satisfied that they were more or less right. That done, we paraded outside and marched to breakfast.

Fulwood Barracks. Our barrack room. The author is second from the right on the front row.

Breakfast tasted super: hot, delicious porridge, followed by bacon and eggs and fried bread, and the usual pint mug of scalding strong army tea. The food at Fulwood was always excellent and we had plenty of it: just as well since we always seemed famished.

Though allowed to walk back we did not delay. We had been given a time by which to return and we knew we had much cleaning to do before first parade at 8.00 a.m. However we just about had time to visit the lavatories at the back of our living quarters and then get ourselves up to the barrack room where detailed instructions were soon being issued for the daily cleaning of our quarters. The floor had to be polished and 'bumped' daily with an odd looking contraption called a floor bumper. I have no idea whether it was some sort of army thing or some sort of Lancashire thing but I had never seen anything quite like it. We cleaned the windows and washed the stairs. We raked out and re-set the fire. And the indoor lavatory on the stair half landing (only to be used in the dead of night and not otherwise) had to be made spotless. We went about our tasks with frantic energy urged on by the lance corporal. At about two minutes to eight we had more or less finished, already feeling exhausted with a whole day ahead of us.

'Stand by your beds, berets on.' We stood in silence and waited.

Then a new voice, a rasping, harsh, sound, compelling and urgent in tone, came up from below:

'GET OUTSIDE ON PARADE!'

It was the voice of someone we had yet to meet: the platoon sergeant, Sergeant Griffiths. We sped down the stairs and quickly joined our downstairs mates who inevitably always arrived first.

'Fall in, in threes!' shouted the corporal and, as we did not know what that meant, he pushed and shoved, and shuffled us into place on the roadway in front of our door, alongside the square.

The sergeant stood silently and menacingly in front of us, impressive with his huge scarlet sash draped across one shoulder and diagonally across his chest. He carried a long intimidating stick, which for the moment he held to the ground like a staff.

'Stand to attention!' screamed Bowerbank, 'shoulders back!'

Sergeant Griffiths looked a good bit older than the corporals; he certainly seemed old to us, and quite terrifying in appearance with a strong granite-like face. Indeed, we held the sergeant in awe throughout our training period. As well as the three tapes, I noticed on his sleeve the impressive wings of a parachutist. This man would take almost complete control of our lives, the two corporals already fading into insignificance in the role of junior assistants.

'When I give the order you will stand at ease,' he growled in what was almost but not quite a shout. 'Corporal Bowerbank: come to attention.'

The corporal demonstrated, lifting his knee high and banging in his boot with a crash to the ground.

'Now, stand at ease,' said the sergeant in a normal voice. The corporal obliged in impeccable fashion.

'Remember,' said Griffiths for our benefit, 'lift your foot off the ground, knee raised high, and hands behind your back.' He laid his stick on the ground and he demonstrated again with perfect precision.

'NOW STAND AT – wait for it – EASE!' he roared, and all of us, including the corporals in front stood, more or less, at ease.

'As you WERE!' he shouted. We shuffled back to attention.

'Wait for the word of command: lift your feet,' and he demonstrated again.

We tried again, and after a few attempts started to get it approximately right. Thus began ten weeks of tough and relentless drill training. We were pretty bad that first time I am quite sure, but we had made a start.

Then, with us standing at ease, an introductory pep talk began, as the sergeant began his daunting task of turning us into soldiers.

It would take ten weeks, he pointed out, because we were infantrymen, the backbone of the Army, unlike the Royal Signals, or Engineers or other corps who got away with a mere six. We belonged to a proud and famous regiment. Later, as trained soldiers, we should join the battalion in Hong Kong, and begin to enjoy life. But we had first to pass all the tests of basic training: drill, weapon training, physical fitness training, before we could pass out and, given the state we were in now, it would be a miracle if we avoided being back-squadded and having to do it all again. Some miserable bums never passed out at all and spent their whole service in the depôt cleaning out latrines. But if we played fair by him, and worked hard, he would play fair by us and he would see that we became first-class trained soldiers, and we should pass out.

He then made it clear that, being totally unfit to be seen on the square, we must march to an area behind the barrack blocks, and learn some of the very basic things, before he could let anyone see us on the parade square. After all, he pointed out, he had his reputation to think of, not to mention the reputation of the East Lancashires.

Round the back we then marched to begin the morning's drill. Lining up in threes, open order march, close order march, coming to attention, standing at ease, stand easy, and how to fall out in the correct manner. We practised with urgency and a good deal of shouting by the NCOs. We found it very new and wearing, and we never satisfied them, or so it seemed in those early days. And of course there were three of them, so we had no chance of escaping their practised eyes and relentless energy. Our boots seemed very heavy on that first day of drill and after the hour we already felt exhausted at 9.00 a.m. And we had been on the go since 6.00! I think we all felt a bit of real despair at that moment as we pondered the thought of having ten weeks of this! What had we done to deserve it? Who did these people think they were to treat us like this?

The lecture next on the agenda gave us a bit of welcome respite from the physical exertions, while we sat. We heard lectures of one sort or another every day during training on health, army infantry tactics, the history of the regiment, and many other topics.

Then came a welcome NAAFI break, with a cup of tea, relaxation, a smoke (we smoked a lot in those days) and then we marched to our barrack room for our PT kit.

'You're going to the gym,' said the corporal.

'Right! Outside, PT kit under your arm. Fall in. By the left, quick march!' Corporal Bowerbank took charge: the sergeant had gone to ground.

As soon as we entered the changing room, a small, wiry, but quite old WO2 (Warrant Officer Class II) from the PT Corps met us. He immediately took control and told us that when he gave the word we must change promptly, and get ourselves into the gym. The last man in would do some press-ups. Our kit when we took it off must be arranged in the correct way, all folded very neatly in a small pile with the belt curled in a circle on top.

'Anyone leaving it in sloppy fashion will end up on fatigues: now move,' he screamed, like a thing possessed.

We rushed to undress, arrange kit, and get into the gym. Inside, wearing shorts and red striped jerseys were the PTIs, all young lance corporals, and all looking lithe and extremely fit. I saw at least half a dozen of them so we had no chance of skiving. The gym reminded me of the gym at school, with wall-bars all around, beams down from the ceiling, various vaulting horses and boxes, ropes and window ladders and such. However, though the gym may have looked like gyms of the past, the activity we had to undertake certainly had no precedents in my memory. We had to race around; we had to hang from wall-bars, and raise our legs to a horizontal position over and over again till they were weary and painful. We had to do endless press-ups and hang from the beam and raise ourselves from the floor by the strength of our arm muscles alone. It felt agonising, and if anyone flagged a PT corporal close by watched and urged him on. The WO2 did nothing, except stand in his black tracksuit, making sure everyone worked to the maximum.

We staggered out at the end of the session with aching limbs and with sweat streaming down our red faces. We had thought that the drill had exhausted us; now we were just beginning to experience real exhaustion.

'You have two minutes to get changed,' screamed Corporal Bowerbank.

'Fall in, in threes, by the left, quick march, left, right, left, right.'

After returning to the barrack room to deposit our PT kit, we lay on our beds for a few desperate minutes before dragging ourselves up to march down to the cookhouse for our midday meal.

As we ate the excellent cooked meal, followed by a pudding, and the usual pint mug of scalding tea, we were in a state of real shock. We had been up since 6.00 a.m., cleaned up the whole place, marched, drilled and had a mad PT session. Though aching and worn out we knew our day had reached only the halfway point. We walked back fairly miserably and had another short period of respite lying on our beds.

Then, we heard it again, the inevitable roar from below: 'GET OUTSIDE ON PARADE!'

The second session of drill began. We practised again the work done that morning (open order march, close order march, stand at ease) for one whole hour: well, not quite an hour because a new man had arrived on the scene, a commissioned officer, Second Lieutenant J.G. Willcox complete with Sam Browne belt, one pip on each shoulder, and a short swagger stick.

He was young, perhaps 20, public school of course: officers just had to be in those days, especially in fighting regiments. He wore a peaked cap, and had hair just a little too long at the back but acceptable in officers. At first he stood and watched, wandering around behind us, then back to the front. Occasionally he would interject something in his cut-glass, highly cultivated voice. He seemed decent enough, but we saw him as a mere schoolboy and a good year or so younger than we were at that.

During a halt, he spoke to us. As our platoon officer he would be interviewing each of us individually in due course. If ever we had any problems we could always go to him: problems at home, anything.

'Right! Carry on s'arnt.'

'Sir!'

The sergeant came to attention and saluted with wonderful style. Mr Willcox returned the salute in that languid way that somehow went with commissioned rank, and he left.

Sergeant Griffiths then explained the real situation. Mr Willcox meant well but he was not the man to help us. If we had trouble at home and needed compassionate leave he, the sergeant, would have a travel warrant and special leave arranged in a flash in a genuine case. Senior NCOs could organise anything quicker than any young officer. We could rely on that!

Following that second drill of the day, instead of the lecture which we half expected they marched us off for intelligence tests. Bits of wire had to be arranged, questions answered, and a great number of problems solved. The Army needed such information in order to work out what we should do after basic training. They took our photographs and dealt with various administrative things like the issue of pay books (AB 64s).

After that period of calm, to our great dismay we learned it was time for the second PT session of the day! We now realised that recruits suffered two sessions of drill and two sessions of PT each day for ten weeks. We should either be the fittest men in Preston by then, or dead. Once again we leapt into action, and undressed in the required two minutes, laying out all our clothes in perfect order. The session had all the violent activity of the morning session and every muscle ached painfully as we marched wearily down for our evening meal at 5 o'clock.

At about 6.00 we returned to the barrack room. The lance corporal gave orders to light the fire which was soon crackling and hissing with flames licking around the coal: that fire seemed the one cheerful thing in our lives at that moment.

Suddenly, Corporal Bowerbank appeared at the door. He had brought the lads from the other rooms with him, so that he personally could set us off on the right lines.

'Have you got your blanco and brush?' He yelled in friendly fashion, to one of our number.

Corporal Bowerbank had two personae. One he displayed on the parade ground: harsh, firm, though always with a touch of friendly humour and conducted with a sort of metaphorical wink, as if to say: 'Come on now, don't take it too seriously. We've all been through it. See the funny side.' The other was the persona of the barrack room after hours, still the boss, always treated with respect, but, human, joking, friendly, and likeable. We could talk to him, ask him questions.

'Yes, corporal.'

'Let's be having it then.'

He demonstrated with one of our filthy belts. The green blanco was like a hard cake of soap, and he rubbed the wet, hard miniature scrubbing brush into it, and then onto the webbing of the belt which began to turn a fresh shade of green.

'That's the way to do all your webbing, gaiters, top-kit as well. Now, see these brasses?'

He fingered the brass fastenings on the belt, and the brass buckles at the back of the belt.

'These have to be gleaming every day! You must clean them every night! They must shine. And no bits of dry white Brasso on them! You need two cloths, one to put the Brasso on, and one to polish it off. Heaven help you if at inspection we see the slightest blemish on those brasses. And clean every brass button on that greatcoat too. And pay particular attention to those cap badges!'

He glared at one of the men from his own barrack room.

'You! Go down and fetch up my top-kit. At the double!'

He leapt to his feet: 'Where is it, corporal?'

Bowerbank went into his mock-fury mode:

'Where is it? Where is it? Best top-kit in the regiment, and you're asking where is it? Haven't you seen it? Haven't you admired it? It's on top of my bloody locker!'

'Yes, corporal!'

We all examined the corporal's top-kit: impeccable, perfect in every way.

'If I can do it, you can do it. I have to keep my kit up to the mark, and you will too. Got that?'

'Yes, corporal,' we chorused.

'And remember those boots: yours are filthy,' he screamed, pointing at those nearest to him.

'Remember, a bit of water in the lid, a bit of polish, not too much or it won't shine, and circular movements with your finger, every night till they look like glass. Isn't that right, Corporal Cottam?'

'Dead right!' agreed his fellow NCO.

The others left for their barrack rooms, and we, having collected our cleaning materials, purchased in the NAAFI the night before, began to get to work on our belts, gaiters, and cap badges.

'You've just got to do a bit every night,' said Lance Corporal Cottam. 'In three weeks' time there'll be a big inspection, and if you pass, and every bit of kit's perfect you might just be allowed out for the first time, and you might even get a brief leave to visit home.'

A brief leave: three weeks! Would any of us survive another day like today, never mind three weeks? Still, the prospect of the carrot had been presented to us: a brief leave. The Army seemed fond of carrots and sticks.

And so as we sat on the floor, around the fire, we began scrubbing the blanco on all our kit, and then left it to dry. And then we started on the boots: the working everyday boots, and the 'best boots', burning off the pimples with the hot spoon, then polishing and polishing in small circular movements with our index fingers pressed inside the duster, and gradually it began to take effect. We found it almost comforting, to clean our kit, after the exertions of the day.

After a while, at around 9 o'clock, the lance corporal said we could go down to the NAAFI for half an hour before bed at 10.00. We approached it with something near to joy and once more the familiar strains of Paul Anka could be heard as we entered the door.

We had some tea but nothing to eat. After that enormous evening meal none of us felt particularly hungry, just absolutely whacked, after a frenetic day of activity. Again we exchanged views on our experiences, about those sessions in the gym, and why on earth had we to get changed in an impossibly short time? And why did our stuff have to be laid out like that? With all this bull how had we ever won the war? And Sergeant Griffiths: what a hard case he was! And what about all that stuff about 'open order march, fall out, and squa-ad SHUN'? Shall we ever master it? We got quite heated about everything that had happened that day but looking back, the most notable thing was that we had begun to become a close-knit group of friends, yet we had known each other only for a day and a half.

'We're going to have trouble with him!'

'Who?'

'Griffiths!'

'He's a right shit!' said someone else with an unusual burst of army language. Up till then none of us had sworn.

'I'd like to meet him one day when all this is over.'

'Never mind all that, just think of now and mind none of us gets back-squadded.'

Eventually we wandered back, a bit depressed, and extraordinarily worn out both mentally and physically.

Soon I lay again in that comfortable bed, in the silent room with the fire flickering and casting shadows on the walls. I hoped I could lie awake for ages and enjoy the luxury of the warmth and the peace, but I fell asleep instantly.

* * *

The pattern had now been fixed, and that first full day repeated again and again. Every day would be filled with exhausting activity: twice-daily PT, cleaning the room, bulling kit, marching everywhere. Drill formed the nub of it all. A move would be impeccably demonstrated. We'd try it (not too well usually) calling out, in the style of recruits, the numbers ONE, TWO, THREE to help our movements. Then we'd have to repeat it again and again till we got it right, and could hear those boots crashing down in unison.

We felt restless, however, and resentful in those first early days. None of us wanted to adapt to this strange, painful, new, way of life. Indeed, after two or three days, rebellion began to stir in our ranks. To us 'sophisticated graduates', as we in our naivety undoubtedly thought ourselves, this all represented some sort of regression. After all, were we not educated, thinking people, who had written essays, conducted seminars, and marched in protest against Suez? Why should we be expected to tolerate this basic training torture? We wanted none of it! We would not put up with it.

And one evening, when the corporals felt us fit to be left alone to get on with our kit cleaning, while they went off to the corporals' mess, we began to plot.

'We must just refuse to do these things, and at the same time, each one of us must write to our MPs: they probably do not realise what is going on!'

'Mrs Bessie Braddock is famous for defending national servicemen, isn't she?'

'Yes, but we must write to our *own MPs*, not Bessie Braddock.'

'Yes, that's right, our own MPs, or maybe the newspapers?'

Moreover we agreed that we should start our new approach the next day when the lance corporal marched us round the back for our drill training. We'd deliberately wheel to the left if he said 'right wheel' and make a deliberate shambles of any drill moves he gave.

On the following day, we carried out the plan to some considerable effect indeed as they led us round to the back. The lance corporal quickly and angrily brought us back in line, but we thought we had made a good point, and felt quite pleased with ourselves. We had made a start in fighting for our rights!

Somehow in our naïve way, we did not think he would report the matter to Sergeant Griffiths, but of course he did!

And the sergeant's fury terrified us. He berated us fiercely, expressing total contempt for what he called our 'soft, civvy street, American way of life, *Daily Mirror,* Bessie Braddock attitudes!' We needed discipline. We needed to learn some lessons. And we were in the right place to receive them. He must have gone on for a full five minutes and then, for the rest of drill period we marched, and double marched, and right wheeled, and left wheeled, relentlessly without pause. We knew then we had lost. We did not have the stomach to take on Sergeant Griffiths, let alone the might of the British Army which he represented. In that key moment our rebellion ended and we had learned a crucial lesson. We never wrote those letters to the MPs and never spoke of them again. Without precisely realising it, I think we all came to the view that we could not beat them, and so we had better join them. As the long weeks continued we stopped grumbling amongst ourselves. We began to swear a bit more when frustrated, and began to see the funny side of things. We started to laugh at our failings and ourselves. Eventually we began to take some pride in achievement. Above all we grew closer as a group, helping each other to adapt, and survive, and even to enjoy to a degree this new way of life that had been thrust upon us and which we just had to learn to live with.

Such developments would take time: meanwhile we desperately looked forward to our first weekend. Was ever a weekend savoured so much? We had to use part of that first Saturday afternoon having army haircuts, and also having army medical injections.

The Army believed in vaccinating its recruits against just about everything. The worst jab, against tetanus, left each man with a painful arm for a day or so. We were glad however not to be the unfortunate lad who got two jabs by mistake. After being jabbed you had to step smartly away. He failed to step away with sufficient alacrity and, the MO having turned to refill his syringe, turned back and gave him a second dose. The boy felt quite ill in the night, but recovered fairly rapidly thereafter. Sunday however was blissful, an all too brief period of respite giving us time to catch our breath and lick our wounds. We also attended a pay parade, after a quick lesson in saluting because we had to march up, come to attention, salute, turn right, and march away. The derisory pay, far less than the pay of regulars, had been money well earned.

During the second week our pain continued but it helped that, after some days drilling behind the barrack block, we finally made it to that 'holy of holies', the square.

They then introduced us a very short time later to a new development in our training.

'Outside on parade!'

It was Corporal Bowerbank's voice, sounding exasperated as usual, but somehow always less menacing than that of the sergeant.

Soon we made a brief march to Fulwood's small indoor range, and our spirits rose in anticipation.

The fairly small range, perhaps 15 feet wide and 50 feet long, had just room for us to crowd in at the near end. At the far end we saw some small, interesting looking targets to shoot at.

'We're going to have a go with the small .22 rifle, before you are let loose on your regular weapon, the .303. The .22 is much lighter and has no kick when you fire it. So it's a good weapon to start on.'

He loaded a rifle, and lay down and demonstrated.

'Press it into your shoulder like this, and remember, never, never point a rifle at anybody, even if you think it's not loaded.'

He pointed it towards the target and fired. The report was sharp, and he hit the bull each time. Lance Corporal Cottam then took his turn with the same impressive accuracy.

We all then enjoyed a bit of shooting, not with a great deal of success at first it has to be admitted, but the corporals made encouraging comments. We found it the most interesting thing so far, and we all had a sense of pleasure and achievement, even though we were only firing .22 rifles.

'Are you going to do your lighted match trick, corporal?' asked Lance Corporal Cottam.

'No! No time!'

'Ah! Go on, corporal, don't be a spoilsport,' said someone.

'Yes, go on,' we echoed.

'All right then, you've talked me into it. Set it up.'

We were all intrigued. At the target end, Lance Corporal Cottam set up a cigarette, with a live matchstick stuck into the top. Corporal Bowerbank lay down with his rifle. With great confidence, he pulled the trigger. After a sharp report, the match head burst into flames as we burst into spontaneous applause.

'Do it again!' we shouted.

'No fear,' said Bowerbank, 'first rule of the Army: quit while you're ahead!'

And then came the second weekend. We worked on Saturday mornings of course and we could not leave barracks at all, but those early weekends were sheer joy for us. We had time for a bath, and a bit of lazing around. We could wander around the camp. We could even fit in a half-hour to visit the tiny TV room to watch, in black and white, 'Six-Five-Special', and we had slightly longer weekend visits to the NAAFI where Paul Anka continued as ever, in his own inimitable style, to entertain the Fulwood recruits.

As each weekend arrived, we watched all those groups ahead of us appearing suddenly, denims discarded, in their well-pressed BD and best boots. After passing inspection at the guardroom those fortunate souls would set off for town, the pictures or the pub. But our turn would come and we knew that, after the first three weeks, we too should be allowed out of barracks. A new intake would then arrive, and Bhurtpore Platoon would no longer be the new boys. How we looked forward, with more than a little bit of optimism, to that coming event.

Time moved slowly, and painfully, days consumed in drill, and PT, and all that cleaning, and bulling. We made progress, however. Marching down to breakfast and cleaning the place frantically became second nature. We began to find twice daily drill and twice daily PT almost normal, well, by the end of the second week anyway.

* * *

By the beginning of the third week we had been it seemed at Fulwood all our lives: we had never seen outside it, but we had no time to think about that. We lived in our own little world ruled by the subaltern and the NCOs. We began to take pride in our kit which looked almost as good as that of the corporals. We were in the Army and resigned to it. The end of that third week, however, now came into sight. We should be allowed out, and should get a brief leave and in that third week we thought of little else. Our BD never yet worn came back from the regimental tailors with all necessary alterations completed and the words 'East Lancashire' in red had been stitched in the correct place at the top of each arm above the red rose flash of the Lancashire Brigade. Friday night saw much activity with iron, water, and brown paper, as we pressed our BD to perfection, instructed by our young 19-year-old lance corporal! Young men did no ironing in those days except on national service, and we were novices! We learned quickly however: getting away on our brief leave would depend upon it.

On Saturday morning we laid out our kit, in good order by then, for full inspection, and out of our working denims and in battledress at last, we stood by our beds, ready to come to attention when Second Lieutenant John Willcox and Sergeant Griffiths entered to inspect the troops. We knew that we had to pass inspection to be allowed out of the barracks. Every item of kit had to be perfect for these weekly full inspections. The locker too had to be perfect.

During the inspection, everybody seemed to have his tie pulled a bit here, or a beret ever so slightly straightened there, or there might be some flicking away of a piece of imaginary dust from an arm, by the young officer as he came round his men. We were about to leave the barracks so they paid particular attention to our appearance and us. Then they pronounced themselves satisfied, wished us well, and reminded us that we were wearing our best BD with 'East Lancashire' inscribed upon our arms, and we must wear it with pride and be worthy of it.

Soon, armed with travel warrants, we passed through that gate for the first time in three weeks, and we saw Preston for the first time from the windows of the bus that took us to the station. We had a tremendous feeling of freedom, at last.

Of course we were not an unusual sight to the people outside. In the 1950s almost every young man did national service. Nearly every male had been in one of the services and many had served in the War which had ended only a decade earlier. Every woman had a father or son or brother or boy-friend or husband, who was in or had been in the services. It was a common sight to see young servicemen in uniform on the streets, and people behaved amiably towards them, and would almost always offer a lift to a hitching soldier, sailor, or airman. We had no need to hitch a lift however on this occasion: we had our travel warrants for this particular leave, a very brief leave of 36 hours but a leave more welcome to us than any words can describe.

I found going home an odd experience though. I had been at Fulwood three weeks and people probably thought: 'He's only been gone five minutes, and he's back already.' But I felt I had been absent for months. Civilian life already seemed far away. How could one tell these people what we had all been through? They would never understand. And although one dreaded going back, in a way one wanted to get back, back to those new friends who really did understand what it was all about. Also I wanted now to get the training finished, and get on with the two years and get it all out of the way, once and for all. And, I really did want to get back, and see that new intake enter that dining-room for the first time.

* * *

2

Metamorphosis

I returned to Fulwood with a happy feeling that, bad as it might have been, the first period of initial shock had ended. I no longer faced the unknown. The frantic days continued but we fit young men were getting fitter every day, and visibly changing. Our denims and shirts after their weekly laundering seemed to be getting a more comfortable worn look, as did our shrunken berets. The boots had not only become easier to wear but also now looked like real army boots, moulded somehow to our feet. Most of all I could see a change in the faces of my fellow recruits: thinner, paler, though also, a bit strained: leaner I suppose would be a good word to describe the metamorphosis. I could see it too in my own face as I looked at it every morning in the mirror above the washbasin. Our clipped army haircuts helped also to develop that same look. I remember having one of those official army photographs taken for identity purposes. We had to hold in front of our chests a metal contraption on which metal figures could be slotted, in this case our army numbers. When I saw the photograph, I thought I was looking at a convict: no beret, clipped hair, gaunt face and holding up the number 23418269. The number of course has become engraved in my memory. They said we should never forget it, and they were right. Every letter I wrote had the number at the top:

23418269 Pte Kelly J
Bhurtpore Platoon
East Lancashire Regiment
Fulwood Barracks
Preston
Lancashire

And every day it seemed, someone would shout, 'Name and number?'

'23418269 Private Kelly J. Sir!' would come the reply.

On our return they deemed us sufficiently experienced to undertake dreaded guard duty: something awful that we had to learn to endure. The duty started in the early evening, after normal training, and continued all night with two hours on, and four hours off. We had to dress up in BD and, as the weather grew colder, gloves and greatcoats. After the short guard mounting parade, one man took his position at the gate; others had to patrol the grounds. During the off duty period in the guardroom we could get a little bit of what everybody called 'kip', but had to remain fully clothed. Then, after hardly any sleep, a full day's work followed.

At that time we suffered a scare concerning the IRA which had become active once again, and had successfully raided one particular army camp to steal arms. Those camps out in the countryside seemed the most vulnerable. Fulwood with its high walls appeared fairly safe, but they did start arming the guard, and guard duty became a bit more than a formality, though they did not arm us recruits.

Another duty involved fire piquet which lasted from 6.00 p.m. to 6.00 a.m., and we learned with surprise one night that the person on fire piquet duty had to sleep with a box of live ammunition under his bed, ready for any emergencies that might have arisen during that period of IRA activity.

Meanwhile the daily drill continued, led by Sergeant Griffiths. The corporals and Mr Willcox were always there too. Though tough, the Army made it interesting, because of the constant new challenges introduced. Our first challenge had been to get onto the square. And then of course we had to stick at first very closely to its edge until fit to get right out into the centre! And then we made it at last, fit to go anywhere!

'Swing those arms BACK!'

Our arms hurt in the horizontal position, especially on the back swing.

'Shoulders BACK! You're like a lot of ruptured DUCKS! Get some SWAGGER into it. That's better! Left, right, left, right. Keep those arms moving!'

We had to learn to come to a halt in perfect order. 'Squa-ad HALT!' And we shouted: 'ONE , TWO!' as we all stopped in unison. 'Fall OUT!'

Fulwood Barracks. Marching recruits.

Indeed that shambolic shuffle that passed for our first march to the cookhouse had rapidly become a real march.

'Fall in, in threes. Right DRESS!' and up went our right arms to touch the shoulder of the man to the right of us, to help us achieve absolutely straight lines. 'By the left, quick MARCH!'

The Army training system was psychologically sound. It knew how to impose discipline, but it also knew how to provide those little stages and steps to be achieved bringing reward and pleasure to us all. We always had some further stage to be conquered, and then performed: on the square of course, in full view for all to see and admire.

We moved on to the stage of turning left and right whilst marching. Soon we could do the about turn on the march. We made errors and the NCOs screamed continually.

'AS YOU WERE! You're like a lot of (glance over shoulder to make sure no female person had inadvertently wandered into Fulwood) FUCKING girl guides!'

'Stand STILL! What are you supposed to be doing, the HOKEY fucking COKEY?'

The swearing and cajoling were almost always done with humour, though we did not dare laugh.

Soon we had mastered a whole new set of skills: marching with a rifle: 'Sl-o-o-pe ARMS. Or-d-e-er ARMS.'

At first marching with the rifle proved difficult, it seemed very heavy! But gradually we became used to it, and the old way of swinging both arms began to seem the more difficult way of marching.

'Pre-e-s-e-nt ARMS' (that is hold the rifle out in front as a form of salute) proved very difficult, and many rifles dropped before we mastered that skill too.

Fixing bayonets usually ended in complete disaster, bayonets falling all over the square, but eventually we conquered even that. We perfected normal saluting. 'Longest way up, shortest way down: now try it again!' Then we practised saluting and 'eyes right' on the march; after all we would have to turn eyes right when marching past the senior officer at the passing out parade.

Twice a day, every day, we drilled with Sergeant Griffiths and the corporals. And eventually we had long since forgotten how we had resented learning all this crazy drill. We had become soldiers at last and we knew it. It had been a hard slog, and we took some pride in it.

That huge barrack square at Fulwood looked a remarkable sight during drill sessions. Several squads of the Loyals over on their side marched across the square, turning, right wheeling, and we could hear their orders echoing out in the distance. On our side numerous East Lancashire squads marched and drilled, all at differing stages of progress. NCOs screamed out orders all over that square but somehow we only ever heard those directed at us. At first we had been the novices and we looked admiringly at the two squads ahead of us, envying their style and precision. Then the new recruits coming up behind us entered the square and we watched aghast at their clumsiness.

We could also, after that initial three week period, leave the barracks at weekends. This meant in effect that we went out on Saturday afternoons, and/or Saturday evenings. Sundays became days for lazing around, and we usually had a lie-in, even though it meant missing breakfast. One of our number, the great Elvis fan, informed us that *Loving You* was on at a cinema in town, and that we must all go to see it on Saturday night. And of course we did. We did everything together during that period at Fulwood.

We also mixed a bit with the lads from the other barrack rooms within Bhurtpore Platoon. Some eighteen-year-old grammar schoolboys mainly from Lancashire would call in to see us from the upstairs room opposite. They usually swore in a very grammar school sort of way saying things like 'blood and sand' with real venom! A couple of Lancashire public schoolboys also popped in from time to time to complain and chat and ask what we thought about everything. The two public schoolboys had real enthusiasm for the Army. They talked about 'the corps at school' and knowingly explained military matters to us. They wanted commissions more than anything and planned to apply to WOSB (War Office Selection Board) as soon as they could. We also knew the very ordinary lads mainly from the Preston area, often bewildered, not particularly well educated, but energetic and willing and fairly cheerful. They made up the majority of the platoon.

We graduates must have seemed oddities really: hardly any of us from Lancashire, 21 years old, and with little interest in applying for commissions. We became a very close knit group.

The young Scots lad, Alan Kirkwood from Greenock, kept us entertained by his constant imitation of Eccles from the BBC radio Goon Show. And if ever we learned that we were to go for a cross-country run or any other new activity then we always heard what Eccles thought of the idea. The Yorkshire boy, Hudson, often seemed to be in a bit of a good-humoured and outraged fumble to get ready on time and amused us by his incomprehensible mumblings of gibberish as soon as he had fallen asleep, usually before anyone else. Another good-natured Leeds lad, Jim Gibbons, a superb footballer, spent every Saturday afternoon playing for the depôt team on excellent sports fields just beyond where the Loyals lived; he talked ruefully about the teaching career he wanted to get on with. The soft-spoken and philosophically patient John Jordan came from Birkenhead and talked reasonably about everything, sometimes in an exaggerated Birkenhead accent when he was in the mood. Our local lad, Peter Crawshaw, indulged early on in a mild expletive and was quite unfairly, but with good humour, dubbed 'foul-mouth' by Dave Brown of Clydebank near Glasgow. Dave himself, an erudite and witty left-winger, became a sort of second-in-command to Dave Jeeves. He talked about everything. He wanted our views on economics, politics, Marx, religion, and the Army. We could never entirely forget the university seminar as long as Dave remained on form. Our guitar-playing boy from Wigan, a German graduate, liked Elvis and rock and roll and looked the part. Lawrence Laidlaw, another Scot and something of an absent-minded intellectual, held a degree in chemistry and another in English. Dave Jeeves, a good-humoured leader, kept us all in line and somehow bound everyone together, talking endlessly to everybody, and making sure that no one felt left out in the cold.

The film, *Loving You*, and its theme song can still transport me back to basic training and those far off days of autumn 1957. Paul Anka's *Diana* however, will always be the winner in arousing old Fulwood memories. Every night when we went down to the NAAFI, a little sooner than in those opening weeks, the 18-year-olds who regularly played the juke-box never disappointed us. They made up the vast majority of recruits at Fulwood Barracks, Preston and, again and again they selected Paul Anka's hit record.

The same lad who took us off to see Elvis came from Wigan. We constantly pulled his leg about Wigan Pier, and one Saturday he insisted we all go there to see the pier for ourselves, and have a good meal also at his mother's house. We spent a memorable day and forever after I have had a soft spot for Wigan.

We placed visits to the pub on our weekend agenda too. We enjoyed life more and the weeks moved on relentlessly with what seemed increasing rapidity towards the end of our training. We felt the excitement of joining the battalion in Hong Kong, a prospect constantly dangled before us.

The Army, however, as armies have a habit of doing, then presented us with a real shock.

'Now listen in! The top brass who organise these things have decided that you are all to be re-badged to the Loyals!'

Gasps of horrified amazement came from everyone of us. How could this be! How could they do it to us? We all glanced across the huge square to where the despised Loyal Regiment lived. We had never had anything to do with them! We had never spoken to any of them as far as we knew.

'Why?' someone shouted when the first shock wore off.

'Why SERGEANT!' screamed Griffiths. 'Address me as SERGEANT! What do you think these are, TRAMLINES?' He pointed with a dramatic gesture at the three tapes on his arm.

'We don't know,' he went on in a more conciliatory tone. 'We just carry out instructions. Now stop worrying. It won't make any real difference. You'll stay over here with us. And we'll continue to train you! But take out those cap badges: collect them up corporal. Now put in these Loyals cap badges!'

We felt devastated. It says a lot for the training that we had once rebelled against that we now absolutely hated handing over those East Lancashire cap badges, and showed our relief that at least we could keep our own sergeant and corporals, men we had once upon a time looked upon with more than a little antipathy.

'We won't go to Hong Kong now, Sergeant.'

'No, the Loyals are fighting in Malaya.'

The news stunned us. Hong Kong had sounded just wonderful. Malaya, and fighting the Communist guerrillas, sounded terrifying. I myself had a first cousin who had been killed in Malaya.

We wore those Loyals badges for a day or two. Things no longer seemed the same. We felt miserable. Then, with no explanation at all they told us that for mysterious reasons known only to the great and the good, things had changed back again.

Had it all been a clever ploy to make us love the old East Lancashires? I do not think so, but how we did love the East Lancashires after that, and with what pride we pinned those cap badges back into our berets! The threat to Bhurtpore Platoon had been an ominous one though, and it would return before any of us left Fulwood.

* * *

The East Lancashire Regiment, that we now felt so attached to, was of course closely identified with Fulwood Barracks. Fulwood had its own almost palpable indefinable and individual atmosphere. It could be sensed on approaching the impressive main gate but it increased markedly as one set foot on the square and observed those heavy grey early nineteenth century barrack blocks. There was a World War II, indeed even a World War I 'feel' to the place. The ghosts of those East Lancashire men who had trained at Fulwood and had fought in those terrible early twentieth century conflicts often came to mind, especially as we set about our weapon training business on those dark rainy autumn days of 1957.

On one of those wet days in October, wearing groundsheets over our denims to keep off the rain, the platoon had been marched to the Fulwood armoury. Each of us had been issued with that famous World War I/World War II rifle, the Lee-Enfield .303. It represented an important step for us: the real thing. We knew that national servicemen were actually using such rifles in war at that very moment, in such places as Malaya.

And of course, once we had our rifles, we made a start on all that rifle drill on the square.

Not long after we had started using the rifle for drill, however, they took us into one of those large high roofed, hangar-like buildings behind the barrack block for our first lessons in the use of the rifle as a weapon.

The safety-catch, they stressed, must always be at the safety position when the rifle was not in use. The battle sight could be used rapidly when taken by surprise at close quarters. The leaf sight lifted up vertically and ensured accuracy with long range targets. They explained that the rifle would have to be zeroed to fit each man's eye, and for that reason we must always keep the same weapon. The bolt action would drive the cartridges into the barrel for firing. Then they explained the safety procedure, known as 'easing the springs', to check that no live rounds had been left in the rifle before the end of practice. They stressed safety over and over again.

'During training, never point that rifle at anyone!' They emphasised this in the very serious first session of weapon training with the .303, just as Corporal Bowerbank had stressed it in that early session with the .22. The sergeant now warned of the power of the .303 pointing out that it could penetrate a thick wooden door.

We did no actual shooting during that first practice, but they gave us instruction in how to load the ten rounds of ammunition, and how to avoid jamming the gun, jamming being a hazard with the .303.

That night we received instruction in the mysteries of 4 by 2 (a piece of cloth for cleaning) and the pull-through, and the vital importance of cleaning the rifle each time after firing it, a new chore to add to all the others.

The next day saw us at the main, outdoor, Fulwood range. We only ever fired our rifles lying down full length, and every move we made was carefully explained and fully demonstrated by the corporals and sergeant, each an excellent shot and good teacher. The heavy-duty sound of the weapon when fired sounded quite

Fulwood Barracks. Weapon training.

impressive. The 'kick' impressed too, ramming itself into the shoulder, despite careful instruction about holding the rifle correctly to minimise the effect. They gave lots of details about gently squeezing the trigger while drawing in the breath but the rifle always seemed to leap upwards when fired, spoiling our efforts to hit the target. We enjoyed it though, worked at it daily from then on and gradually improved, aware that eventually we would all be taken out to the distant ranges at Altcar. There we should have to show skill and accuracy over great distances, and also undergo tests to determine whether we became marksmen, or first or second class shots or whatever. If we failed, we would be back-squadded, a terrifying thought for all of us, and a real incentive to work at any weaknesses we might have. As well as shooting the rifle, we inevitably had a session or two running with fixed bayonets at stuffed dummies, though we did it in silence and not with all that macabre screaming that one sees on films about army life.

We also had to work on the light machine gun, known as the l.m.g. or bren gun. The most difficult thing to master was taking it apart, and putting it together again and we spent many hours in a large indoor training area getting the hang of it all, learning the names of the parts and trying to assemble it and take it to pieces in a fixed time while the rain belted down outside. Henry Reed's great poem 'The Naming of Parts' brings it all back to anyone who went through those experiences. Infantrymen had to run with a bren in dismantled pieces, and then set it up for use on a ridge or whatever and later on we did fieldcraft, running around with rifle and l.m.g. but in those early sessions, getting to know the names of those parts, and setting the thing up in the very limited time allowed proved quite a daunting task, and we failed time and time again before eventually mastering it. Firing the bren however seemed easier to me than firing the rifle. Again we had to lie down flat behind the gun, and then load, and fire single shots, then a burst, but because it rested on legs it felt much steadier and did not 'kick' like the rifle.

Then of course we had to master the sten gun, a small hand-held sub-machine gun. When I was a boy, during the War, we boys used to run around playing 'commandos' and 'firing' at each other with toy 'tommy' guns. I suppose the sten must have been a later version of that. It seemed notoriously inaccurate, even at short distances, unlike the rifle which proved exceedingly accurate over vast distances. Nevertheless, I think we all enjoyed firing the sten at carved-out cardboard figures, just a few yards in front of us, once again playing 'commandos'! The sten jammed easily though, and we all froze one day when we heard the Scots voice of Dave Brown saying 'It won't fire Sergeant,' and then watched him swing round towards Sergeant Griffiths, with the weapon pointing straight at Lawrence Laidlaw! The fury and expletives of the sergeant exploded around the small range, though fortunately the sten gun did not.

Well into our training, they gave us a whole day at the ranges at Altcar. Getting out of the barracks, whether for a route march or a cross-country run, or a Saturday night out always made a welcome change, and the trip to the ranges sounded very promising. With some alarm we took down our well blancoed and Brassoed top kit: alarm because we were sure it was now going to be messed up and we should have to clean it all again when we returned! We also took down our mess tins. Then, on the following day, at 8.00 a.m., we set off in one of those three-tonners that had first brought us to Fulwood from Preston station. But on this occasion we felt pleased to be getting into the vehicle, and though the roof was covered over, the back remained open so we could enjoy the view. We had no idea of Altcar's whereabouts, but it seemed a long journey. It passed pleasantly with lots of chat; we were amongst friends after all, unlike that very first silent journey.

On that bright cold day when we stepped out of the truck they divided us into two groups, the first taking first turn in the butts: deep trenches, safely below the huge targets. We approached a long row of these targets, and a couple of us, stationed at each one, had to use long pointers, to indicate to the men shooting where their shots had gone. Each pointer had a large blade at the end, white on one side, and black on the other. We had to watch carefully, and then suddenly of course a shot would land. If it was a 'bull', then we raised the pole (keeping ourselves safely below the parapet) and pointed the white side to touch the bull.

If an 'outer' we pointed the black side to the outer rim of the target, and waved it from side to side. If an 'inner' we pointed to the white side to the target and waved the pole from side to side. If a 'magpie' (between 'inner' and 'outer') then we twirled the pole showing black and white alternately. Being in the butts proved a lot more entertaining than we had anticipated, and we speculated about how we could cheat, and give people better scores than they deserved, but I do not think any of that actually happened. The thought of the terrible punishment that would follow if caught made it too terrifying to contemplate. Anyway they supervised us closely. Each soldier fired several shots with both rifle and l.m.g. and then eventually the real test came at last after the session of practice, and they gave him his final score.

At the shooting end, the targets seemed to be about a mile away; they certainly looked no bigger than the little targets at Fulwood, and yet actually the Altcar targets were huge! We had to run up, throw ourselves down, and shoot, urged on and assisted by the NCOs, who genuinely wanted us to do as well as possible.

At midday we enjoyed an excellent cooked meal at the field kitchen, manned of course by the ACC cooks. We had a savoury meat dish in one mess tin, and rice pudding in the other, and lots of that delicious army tea, complete with its bromide, or so they said.

We all passed the test, mostly becoming first class shots; some became marksmen, each qualified to have a special badge on the sleeve of his BD top.

After that enjoyable day out, we realised that we had all come through an important assessment of our skills, progressing to 'trained soldier' status, and up to the standard we hoped, of all those 'ghosts' who had gone before us at Fulwood, but who, unlike us, had had to go to war in Europe and elsewhere.

That evening we set to work cleaning not only the rifles but also the mess tins, top-kit, boots, all of which, as we had feared, had suffered quite a bit.

* * *

As the weeks passed we continued to have PT twice a day. The two minute dash to get changed became second nature as time went by. And of course we became fitter and fitter and began to enjoy the challenge of it all. We knew that we had to pass all the PT tests: shinning up a rope, raising oneself on the beam, and so on. They constantly made notes on each man's progress. The young PTIs would demonstrate every new skill, while the old WO2 looked on. We saw him as one never satisfied, always complaining, but never actually doing anything himself.

In the later days of training, we had to do a number of things with the box. This included running up, springing into the air, doing a somersault, and then landing perfectly. We always made a hash of it. We would land on the box itself, the somersault always seemed disastrous, and we usually failed to land perfectly to attention. While all this was going on, with the poor lance corporal PTIs doing their best to get something out of us, the WO2, standing there in his black tracksuit, would be screaming abuse.

Suddenly, in the midst of our failure, he called us all to attention.

'What is the matter with you?' he shouted. 'You are not running up correctly. Have confidence in yourselves. And take a proper spring from the board.'

He paused, and then continued, 'Like this!'

And then to our complete astonishment (for he had never ever demonstrated anything and we were convinced that he could not actually do anything) he set off for the box. He sprang into the air, and performed the most perfect somersault imaginable and completed his feat by landing perfectly to attention.

'That's the way to do it. Now get on with it!'

Our view of that old WO2 changed forever!

Day after day we went to that gym, eventually fighting in twos with quarter-staffs and even doing some boxing. As those weeks of training went by, we began to feel better and better after each session and certainly not as weary as in those far off early weeks.

We also did cross-country runs and route marches during which we alternatively ran and marched whilst singing songs like

The Happy Wanderer. The singing would help, they told us, and they were right: it did. These marches took us past something called 'the Preston by-pass' which was under construction, a road that would ultimately become part of the M6.

We also had to run a mile in six minutes in order to pass out, but after all our training no one had any trouble achieving that.

We also had to be able to swim, and for about three weeks we travelled daily to Preston baths where they taught us to swim in efficient army fashion, even though many of us, including me, could actually swim already! It made a wonderful break from our routine in the barracks.

Somewhere in the middle of training everything became disrupted by an outbreak of Asian 'flu. People actually collapsed on the square and fell down on their faces when trying to stand to attention. Anyone trying to help a man who fell faced a severe reprimand. One or two men became bad enough to be put into the Fulwood medical wing, in effect a small hospital at the back of the barracks, beyond the square. Lawrence had been badly affected and, looking even more pale and lean than usual, he had been whipped off to hospital. After a few days we all went anxiously to visit him expecting to find him lying in a desperately weakened state in one of the hospital beds. We looked everywhere but failed to find him till he suddenly appeared carrying a tray of drinks for the patients! The ever-pragmatic Army, finding themselves short-staffed, had turned him into a medical orderly. We fell about laughing; he insisted in his serious Scots way that he needed a good rest. We felt quite envious of his new easy life but he rejoined us within days. And, notwithstanding the 'flu attack, the constant PT had turned us quickly into hardened and fit young men and most of us quickly recovered.

Eventually we had passed most of the tests required in the gym, but we still had one major test to conquer. We had to fulfil the dreaded assault course in a designated time, and then complete it with some accurate target shooting with our rifles. And at last, quite late on in the basic training, they announced that we had become fit enough to attempt it. It would be quite an ordeal, consisting of leaping over water jumps, scaling ropes, climbing obstacles of various sorts, and tackling numerous other difficulties including a huge wall that could only be scaled by two people working together. One stood on the other's shoulders to reach the top of the wall, and then he leaned over to pull the other one up. We also had also several medium sized walls to climb, the last being only about three feet high, but always the most difficult of all because, when we reached that final point we had hardly any more strength to muster. Somehow, we had to drag ourselves over that final obstacle but many failed in that last attempt.

We had several practice attempts but once we had qualified with the rifle we could face our final assault course test. We had to get around the whole thing, carrying the rifle, and then having scaled that last small wall we had to run round to the nearby range, throw ourselves down to the ground, and fire off a series of shots successfully at the target. And it all had to be done within a set time. Most failed the first attempt, and had to tackle it again and again until they succeeded.

Just as we reached increasing physical fitness, we began marching and drilling with increasing confidence during the fourth, fifth and sixth weeks. By the seventh week with two groups behind us we should soon be the senior intake. We felt increasingly confident. One day, a drummer materialised, and we began to march and drill to the drum. Suddenly it had all become much easier: we knew the moves, and could concentrate on achieving a better and better performance. And of course, it began to dawn on us that before long we would march, in full BD rather than denims, at our own passing out parade to the stirring sound of a military band.

Indeed, towards the end of October about three weeks before our turn came, we marched out onto the square, in order to act as markers for the passing out parade of the intake ahead of us. First on, and last off, we had an excellent view of the whole thing: the high table with honoured guests, and the saluting dais where the senior officer would take the salute. Onto the square came the recruits who were passing out, eventually marching past impressively to the stirring tune of that best of all military marches, 'Old Comrades'.

After that Bhurtpore became the senior intake, moving into our eighth and ninth weeks of training. It seemed that we had been at Fulwood Barracks forever! The passing out parade, the peak of our training period, came closer and closer. By that ninth week, we had all passed the tests required of us regarding weapons training, PT, and drill. No one would be back-squadded. We would all pass out. But as the day of our parade drew near we had to practise and practise so that our performance would be up to the mark.

Finally the RSM (Regimental Sergeant Major) appeared and put us through our paces:

'I want none of this business,' said RSM Duffy, demonstrating a particularly sloppy example of coming to attention.

'And none of this business,' he went on, demonstrating something else that he did not like.

He urged us to do our best: this passing out parade was a day to be proud of being in the East Lancashire Regiment. We were going to pass out as trained infantry soldiers. It would be a day to remember. He need not have worried. Sergeant Len Griffiths, one of the best in the business, had trained us and we had begun to look forward to the parade. We had certainly worked, and suffered, over ten of the longest weeks any of us had ever experienced.

Eventually the great day came: Saturday 23 November. We waited, out of sight, ready to go on to the square. Then the parade began. We drilled to perfection, performing every move without error, being inspected at open order, and then marching past to the beat of the drum and the stirring sound of the band, turning eyes right as the salute was taken. Of course presentations were made to the best recruit, and the best shots on rifle, bren gun, sten gun, and not least to the cross-country winner: Jim Gibbons from our very own barrack room.

We had come through it successfully, and we had earned and certainly enjoyed our little bit of glory. Fulwood had a long history dating back to the 1840s, and I suppose many a grand parade had been held on that square, but that day in November 1957 belonged to us, the moment when intake 57/17 took the stage. More than that, we had crossed some sort of Rubicon:

regrets about being called up and all thoughts of grumbling and complaining lay in the past. We had survived. We could and did accept our fate and looked forward to what could be an interesting future.

Time was short, soon the postings would go up, but first Sergeant Griffiths announced that he wanted to arrange a night out for us all, a coach trip to Oldham, with plenty of beer and visits to as many pubs as we could fit in. We were now trained soldiers, and fit to socialise, almost on equal terms with the NCOs. We had come a long way in ten weeks!

It was a great night to remember, with lots of singing all the way back to Preston, the sergeant giving a wonderfully sentimental rendition of one of the old songs: *I'll be your sweetheart.* He seemed quite human! It crossed my mind that soon a new intake would be arriving, and actually moving into our barrack room. Sergeant Griffiths, Corporal Bowerbank, and Lance Corporal Cottam would be going through all that stuff again with a new lot of raw and naïve recruits.

'If only they could see the sergeant now!' I thought. But of course a sight like that has to be earned by ten weeks of slog, and I shuddered at the thought of what they were in for.

The following day they gave us the information we awaited. No one would be flying out to the East Lancashires in Hong Kong because Bhurtpore Platoon would be re-badged after all into the Loyals. Following a short leave, they would embark for Malaya and warfare against the Communist guerrillas. The news came as a shock to us all but to our surprise and relief the ten of us in our particular barrack room did not receive the new cap badges. We learned that our graduate in languages would join the Intelligence Corps in Edinburgh to learn Russian. The rest of us would go to Wilton Park Camp, Beaconsfield, Bucks., to train for eight more weeks, to be army educational instructors.

It had been a remarkable time, not only because it did the impossible and turned us into soldiers in ten short weeks, but also in the often revealing things it taught us about human behaviour. Much took me by surprise during basic training at Fulwood but none more than the remarkable amount of swearing we heard. I was amazed, astounded, and certainly entertained by the swearing, but never I have to say was I offended in the slightest way. All the main swear words were used, but the 'f' word was the endearing one, used in every sentence, and with total lack of meaning!

'You've fucked it up haven't you?' Or, 'What the fuck do you want?' And of course 'Fuckin' hell!' Or just, 'Fuck it!' And, most endearing of all, splitting up the syllables as in: 'You're im-fucking-possible!'

In our barrack room, swearing did not exist at first, and crept in only slowly, and to a limited degree, usually to express real frustration, but we did enjoy hearing it from the NCOs, and often laughed about it, and mimicked it.

We talked little of girls or girl-friends during this basic training period. Perhaps it all seemed too remote in our all-male society, or perhaps there really was bromide in that tea!

Nor was there any homosexual practice. If there had been, we would have known about it: we lived in a close society without secrets. We did indulge however in endless homosexual jokes and some occasionally enjoyed a bit of pretence like mock kissing. Some even pretended jokingly to get into each other's beds, but it all remained harmless fun.

There was however a depth and degree of friendship which I have never experienced elsewhere.

Many words and phrases can be conjured up to catch the mood and feeling of those ten weeks of infantry basic training with the East Lancashires. Everything seemed concentrated: pain, weariness, laughter, fear, expectation, and above all comradeship. The ten of us slept in the same room, washed together, ate together, trained and suffered together, relaxed together. We were hardly ever apart for ten weeks. We hid nothing from each other. We knew each other's weaknesses and strengths. If anyone seemed worried we came to his aid. We helped each other through everything. We became completely honest and trusted each other totally. When it eventually ended, it seemed more like the end of ten months rather than ten weeks and in many ways it was: ten months development and perhaps ten years of friendship crammed into the remarkable intensity of those ten unique weeks.

3

It must be located in the hills

In the 1950s trains still had corridors and little compartments, quite unlike the cattle trucks that were introduced in the following decade, and I sat in one of those compartments on my way to King's Cross London on that early December day in 1957. Each compartment housed a little community; indeed people usually said 'good-bye' to everyone on leaving, often despite sitting for a few hours saying nothing much at all apart from an occasional: 'Do you mind if I open the window a little?'

Sometimes a catalyst in the compartment, usually a woman, started a conversation and soon everyone would be chatting like old friends. This occurred on that particular journey to London.

She nodded in my direction and smiled:

'Off on leave? Or has it just finished?'

'Just finished. I'm off to a new posting, a place called Beaconsfield. I get a train at Marylebone station, if I can find it.'

'Ah, that's a shame, going back I mean. Still, it's a change for you.'

National servicemen too catalysed conversation and soon a long conversation began about the armed forces, people's experiences, and the war, and the journey passed pleasantly.

I backed out of the conversation once I had answered my questions however, and gazed at the little wall light opposite as I pondered my future. Things were not so bad. I had a ten shilling note from my father, pressed into my hand when he had come to see me off. I had not expected it, but it would be very useful: national servicemen were paid little. More important, basic training was over, over and done with, forever! And everyone had always said that that was the hardest time, and anyway I had a lot of army friends now.

I knew nothing of Beaconsfield, nor indeed of the south of England! I had never been to London. I had never been south of Manchester. Nor indeed had anyone of my acquaintance. The north was my country. Scotland too, I suppose, seemed part of my world at that time: we had always gone there for holidays, staying with our Scottish relatives, and I had certainly felt at home with the Scots and the northerners who had made up our barrack room in Preston, but the south seemed a foreign land. It would be an interesting experience getting to know it however, or so I convinced myself, and by the time we reached King's Cross, and had said 'Goodbye' to everyone, I began to look forward to the future.

London disappointed me: the bit I saw looked much like other towns I had seen, though truth to tell, I felt too hot and bothered about negotiating my way to Marylebone to notice much. Then I saw those familiar faces on the platform waiting for the train to Beaconsfield and I immediately felt more relaxed.

We hurried towards our little steam train and piled into a compartment which ran the full width of the carriage: those little local trains had no corridors. Outside I heard:

'Calling at Denham, Gerrards Cross, Seer Green, Beaconsfield ...'

'That's us ... Seer Green, remember; we don't get off at Beaconsfield.'

'Yeah, I wonder why?'

Then doors banged, and we heard a blast on a whistle.

The little train moved off into what I took to be the rural south: trees, hedges, woods, but all looking cold, with no leaves to be seen. The train clickety-clicked its way along, stopping every so often. At each station some one would shout something like 'Gerrards Cross, Gerrards Cross,' doors banged, another loud whistle, and off we puffed again. During the delightful journey we talked about the southern English scenery, about Wilton Park Camp, and what it might hold in store.

Before long the train pulled into Seer Green, and we gathered our kit-bags and alighted at the little rural station. On the platform an army driver met us.

'You the new intake? We've got to go round all the roads. Quicker to walk through the fields.'

'Not with this lot, pal,' said one of us, pointing to the kit-bags.

We travelled down a pleasant country road and soon came to the outskirts of Beaconsfield, passing by some very grand houses.

The truck turned into a long drive and what appeared for all the world like the entrance to a country estate. Eventually we stopped at a barrier marking the entrance to Wilton Park Camp. The barrier lifted, and in we went. Over to the left we saw a large white country house.

'Officers' mess,' said the driver.

Not far ahead we could see various low buildings, and what looked like some round-topped Nissen huts. Everything appeared to be surrounded by trees. We seemed to be in a large wood.

'Well, lads, it looks a lot different from Fulwood Barracks,' said someone, echoing I suppose at that moment the thought of every one of us.

Administrative things out of the way we found that all of us from Fulwood would share the same accommodation: Hut 21. Similar huts to the left and right of us housed newcomers from other infantry regiments. We were all in C Company. Across the pathway to the right stood the ablutions block shared by all C Company huts.

Wilton Park Camp, near Beaconsfield.

We enjoyed an evening meal in the dining/kitchen block. The dining-room was large, and square, and we had to queue up for food as at Fulwood, but in an altogether more subdued atmosphere. And everyone wore BD rather than denims, which gave the place a slightly more sombre feel. Food seemed much less plentiful: perhaps basic training units had a bigger ration allowance.

We returned to our roomy Hut 21 with its curved roof, windows at each end, and rows of typical army beds down each side, each pointing to the centre, and each bed with the usual locker at its side. A handsome old-fashioned stove had a long metal chimney disappearing into the roof. It was cold, but we soon had the stove glowing and crackling: it made an enormous difference turning the place into a cosy retreat from the camp outside. We knew we had to be up early for breakfast and parade

Wilton Park Camp. Barrack huts.

with the company sergeant major, so we turned in early.

I lay for a while in the darkness, illuminated a little by the glow of the stove. Then the silence was broken by the voice of the Yorkshire lad given to occasional incomprehensible mutterings whilst asleep. For once however he spoke out with great clarity:

'It must be located in the hills!'

A few seconds later from another corner came another voice in reply:

'Meanwhile, back at the ranch!'

Laughter echoed through the dark hut followed by silence as we all drifted off to sleep.

Those words would remain something of a catch-phrase which we used again and again during our time at Beaconsfield, guaranteed always to raise a laugh and cheer us up.

* * *

As we sat at breakfast the following morning, we all felt curious about this new period of training upon which we had now embarked. We had a rough idea of what it might be about of course, but what exactly would it involve? What exactly were we training for? We should soon find out.

At 8.30 we settled ourselves in a lecture room, somewhere in the admin. block, which also contained the orderly room, the adjutant's office, and indeed a number of other key offices: the hub of the camp. Here they calculated pay, kept records, revised courses. On that first full day, we all found ourselves sitting in the presence of the two captains who would become our mentors. They later identified themselves as ex-grammar school boys like us, who had taken short service commissions and were now probably in their thirties. They seemed reasonable, sensible, likeable officers: people with whom we could identify.

One of the captains introduced the course, saying that many national servicemen were functionally illiterate and innumerate. The state system of education had failed them and their low educational achievement made it difficult to train them for military duties.

This surprised me quite a bit; indeed we talked about it later that day with some amazement. We had all lived sheltered educational lives in our nice little grammar schools. We hardly knew that other section of the population, 80% or so in fact, who had 'failed' the 11+ and who had received only an elementary education in secondary modern schools. Some of them – quite a lot of them – had had very special needs that clearly had not been catered for.

The captain pointed out that other national servicemen, and regular soldiers too, despite having ability and promise, had also failed the selection test for grammar schools. Far from being illiterate or innumerate however, their particular educational potential had simply remained undeveloped. The system of education had failed them too by not stretching them. They needed to work their way up to the 'O' Level standards of which they were capable. Their promotion would depend upon it.

This again came as news to us. In our naivety and ignorance, we believed that even those in bottom grammar school streams, let alone those who had 'failed' the 11+, could never pass anything as grand as 'O' Level! The Army certainly appeared more optimistic than the world in which we had been brought up.

The job of the RAEC (Royal Army Educational Corps), explained the other officer, was to bring each man up to his potential, achieving in efficient military fashion what the school system had failed to achieve. And we must do it quickly: we did not have the ten years that the schools had had. And soldiers would be able to spend only a small proportion of their time on education; they would still have to do all their other military duties. They presented it as a very appealing and idealistic challenge.

It seems remarkable to me that some people at the beginning of the 21st century actually point to the 1950s and the grammar/secondary modern system as some sort of golden age of high standards for all! They laud the old grammar schools but somehow manage to forget the 80% or so rejected by that system. If people from that era seem well educated today, then quite often it was because of the efforts made by the Army, and not the educational system.

'Any questions?' barked one of the captains, who had a faint Welsh accent.

'Yes, sir, how does it work? Does every soldier get sessions of education?'

'Certainly: a part of every national serviceman's week consists of attending education sessions, unless exempt because of having a good set of 'O' Levels, and there are not many of those.'

'Do we give any training at all for 'O' Levels, sir?'

'Sometimes that's the right thing for a particular soldier; it provides the right incentive, but mostly they will prepare for the Army Certificates of Education third class, second class, and first class, first class being in fact of 'O' Level standard.'

He looked closely at the recruit instructors sitting in front of him.

'Now, if you are successful on this eight week training course – and please note this is a stringent course and you will be expected to work hard – you will then go out to your units, mostly abroad, as sergeant instructors, working with one or two others as a small team. You will enjoy it I am sure; you will be very much part of the regiments and will have all the usual military duties of a sergeant, but you will find yourselves much respected for your main work as educational instructors.'

He paused.

'Yes, you have a question?'

'Yes, sir, are we concerned with maths and English mainly?'

'Maths, English. Current Affairs too. A soldier serving in Cyprus needs to know why we are there. Morale depends upon it. Why are British troops serving in West Germany? Why is Berlin divided? Who are the Communists? The Army produces some excellent pamphlets by the way, and you will find them in our library here at Wilton Park. Look at them. Every unit receives a supply of them. We also teach general studies, which can amount to just about everything and anything.'

That ended the introductory session. Plenty would follow: a long training programme lay ahead. If any of us thought we were back at college then we would have been wrong. Even lectures in the Army had a certain amount of sitting to attention, and coming to attention, and falling out correctly. After all, the whole thing operated within a military establishment, with fatigues, guard duty, PT and parades and above all drill, and that first full day would not pass without a healthy dose of drill.

We had met Company Sergeant Major (CSM) H. Stott of the Irish Guards briefly at the morning parade and that had been quite lively; after the lecture we had a longer session. Stott was tall and incredibly well turned out, wearing a Guards cap with one of those near-vertical peaks that reach right down to the eyes. The intimidating strap lay just above the chin. He had a large moustache and a huge, Irish sounding roar.

'Open ord-e-errr MARCH!'

We obeyed still calling out like recruits: 'One – two – one – two'.

'As you WERE! One – two – one – two. Regiments of the line! Get some life into your movement!'

'Onetwo/onetwo – onetwo/onetwo. Look lively now!'

We got the message: we were mere regiments of the line! But now we were going to do things brigade of guards fashion! And we had thought square bashing more or less over!

'Squa-a-d! Open orderrr MARCH! Onetwo/onetwo!'

'As you WERE!'

We marched, turned left on the march, then right on the march, and then about turned on the march. We halted, and stood to attention banging in our boots, and then we went off again. All the movements we now knew so well were rehearsed again and again. We performed well, I think, but we had to be even better to please the CSM. In eight weeks, we would be made up to the rank of sergeant, and then posted to units with compulsory morning parades, perhaps leading a squad onto the parade ground. Sergeants mounted the guard, and did orderly sergeant duties. We had to be able to perform well and with confidence in front of the men. Eight more weeks of daily drill followed.

Nor did the day end before we suffered another one of those gruelling sessions of PT. Held mainly outside, it consisted mainly of running round the camp, followed by lots of toe touching, trunk bending, running on the spot, and so on.

This did not worry us because Preston had made us incredibly fit. And deep down we knew that this course, though concerned with education, would not resemble our soft university life, which by then had begun to seem a bit decadent. We had become used to a day with lots of change and plenty of movement and physical activity. Before call-up a day of lectures and writing would have seemed normal; now we needed to get out and actually do something physical every day.

That night, after our evening meal, we returned to our hut, lit the stove, and set about cleaning everything for the inevitable inspection on Saturday morning. Indeed inspections could come at any time and we always had to be ready. We also chose our hut orderly as instructed. He would take charge and allocate duties, and call the hut to attention on the day of inspection, though remaining like the rest of us a mere private soldier, or recruit-instructor, as we were henceforth, rather grandly, to be known.

We had scarcely settled into Wilton Park and its ways before Friday came. The time for our final preparations for our first big Saturday inspection arrived. We approached the coming event

with appropriate seriousness and cleaned everything on Friday night, including the hut, and pressed our BD. Top-kit, webbing, boots, in fact every item of equipment down to knife, fork and spoon would be scrutinised minutely. On Saturday morning we laid out our smaller items, on the bed, below our squared off blankets and sheets. The Chief Instructor, Lieutenant Colonel F.K. Hughes would carry out the inspection.

We felt nervous; the Chief Instructor proved unrelentingly strict, a perfectionist. I suppose he took the view, quite rightly, that we were very privileged to be in line for promotion to sergeant after only a few months in the Army: normally it would take ten years to reach that rank. In return for such rapid progress we had to progress rapidly ourselves and no sloppiness would be tolerated. A retinue of officers would accompany him, and once they reached C Company, our own CSM would join them.

The following morning, after breakfast, we set about our remaining tasks with a will; we had been well trained at Fulwood. We cleaned the stove, and whitened its surround, checked finally that everything was in order, including each other's dress –

berets, belts, ties – and then stood by our beds. We caught a glimpse of the retinue of officers now and then as they went from hut to hut, gradually getting closer to us.

As they approached the door and entered Hut 21, our hut orderly came to attention and called out:

'Hu-ut, SHUN!'

And the inspection began. As the Chief Instructor looked closely at the first soldier, his colleagues seemed to buzz around the bed like bees, picking up and examining everything. Someone else glanced in the locker. Others would be examining the stove and the windows.

They found fault with forks, belts, mugs, windows, just about everything, but they seemed to be the usual small faults that they always found: we should survive.

Lieutenant Colonel Hughes gave a final hostile glare at everyone.

'Right, orderly, stand them at ease!'

'Sir!' and he saluted.

'Hu-ut, stand at, EASE!'

In a way, we felt very flattered that we, and the state of our hut, and our own appearance counted for so much. We mattered.

Beaconsfield in the 1950s.

Many more inspections followed: every week in fact. But for the moment we had survived. We had earned the right to go out, look at Beaconsfield, and relax.

After our Saturday midday meal we left the camp, and set off to walk down that long drive and into the High Street. It looked a charming south of England sort of place, with delightful pubs to visit and teashops, which we did not visit. Beaconsfield's black and white timbered buildings looked both pretty and picturesque. Later on, after our evening meal, we went down there again, visiting the pubs, and returning slightly the worse for wear, but well enough to pass muster at the gate. This became quite a regular weekend pastime, always restricted however by our shortage of money.

On Sunday morning, a couple of us decided to go to communion service at the parish church at the main crossroads in Beaconsfield. The impressive church had a large congregation, and we enjoyed being away from the Army atmosphere for a while. We stood out of course in our uniforms, and people made quite a fuss.

'Do come to the parish breakfast! It's only toast and marmalade but it does give us a chance for a chat and a get-together.'

Church ladies busily poured tea and buttered toast.

'Now, what are your names, and where are you from?'

'From the north.'

'From Scotland.'

'Really! I have a son in the north, in Manchester. Now, I'm Lady Burnham. I live in the large house just beyond the corner. You can't miss it. If ever you can get away, or if you are at a loose end, I want you to call in, and have tea.'

She sounded charming, very much of the south of England, and very upper class I thought, but none the worse for that. We never returned to the church; it just seemed too much hassle getting up early after a hard week, and we did not call in at Lady Burnham's for tea, but I often wish that I had. We later visited Burnham Beeches, well known woods not far away, and I thought they must have had some connection with her family.

That was the first of many pleasant weekends at Wilton Park Camp and Beaconsfield. In those that followed we discovered that by hitch-hiking we could open up all sorts of possibilities and get farther afield.

* * *

Essentially our mentors at Wilton Park aimed at perfecting our skills as instructors. We had only about eight full weeks in which to train, and they set a cracking pace, wasting no time. We had to master the mechanics of instruction and rapidly at that.

They placed quite a lot of emphasis on mathematics teaching. We could all *do* basic mathematics of course. After all, we had all passed 'O' Level mathematics only a few years earlier, or the Army would never have selected us for that course. To instruct young soldiers, however, we needed also to *understand* mathematics, and they correctly assumed at Wilton Park that we probably had more than a few weaknesses in that department. After all, most grammar schools merely taught the tricks of the trade. We knew for instance that, when we divided two thirds by three quarters, we put down two thirds, changed the divide sign to multiply, turned the three quarters upside down, and then got on with it. But why? No one at school had bothered to explain that! No one explained the relationship between vulgar fractions and decimal fractions, or why, given a vulgar fraction like four fifths, you could divide five into four, putting a point after the four and you would get a decimal fraction? And what was a decimal anyway? And why do two minuses when multiplied give a plus? The course at Beaconsfield paid much attention to all these matters.

They encouraged us to perform the processes in new common-sense ways, avoiding the 'tricks' we had been taught at school. Subtracting 137 from 211, we should say: 'Well 100 from 200 is 100; then take away 30 leaving 70. Then take the 7 from the 11 leaving 4; so the answer is 74'.

This made more sense than, '7 from 1 won't go, so borrow 10 and then pay it back' and so on, which we had all learnt at school, and which had been a lot of nonsense really even if it did get the right answer. And yet our grammar schools had indoctrinated us so much that we resisted at first, just as we had resisted at first at Preston:

'What is the point of all that? What was he going on about? What use is all that? Why cannot we just teach them how to get the answer?'

We were wrong, of course. Most people will learn only when they understand, especially those who have failed at school. The best way to teach soldiers to whom number remains a frightening mystery is to catch their interest, and demystify things by careful and clear explanation. Time and experience would teach us all that: meanwhile army discipline ensured that we learned the correct way forward whether we wanted to or not, and in that first week and also during the several weeks that followed, we spent time learning the proper approach to mathematics.

The Army way of teaching, involving clarity of explanation and a need to show the soldier that it all made sense, applied to English skills as well as to mathematical skills. Correct English is common sense: that was the message. Say what you mean; mean what you say. We knew what correct English was: the old grammar schools knew all that, but the rules were really common sense in action. Gradually, after thinking it all through, we became confident that we could improve their English however bad it might be.

I suspect that we should find English difficult to teach today because common-sense has been abolished and illogical meaningless English has become politically correct, and is now practised even by prime ministers.

e.g. Each person should drive THEIR car carefully.

e.g. Every doctor should ask THEMSELVES what THEY are aiming at.

e.g. They should all bring their WIFE with them.

Instructors in good English can no longer appeal to common sense and logic. They can appeal only to the shifting sands of political correctness. And if sloppiness becomes the rule, who can say which particular piece of sloppiness is right? Those pusillanimous people who are so terrified of what feminists might say if they even think about using the word 'his' have not only rendered our language meaningless but also made teaching it difficult, if not impossible. Fortunately for us, we had no such problems in the late 1950s.

General studies and current affairs also played a crucial part of the courses we would teach, and we knew very little about those. To get us all involved with general studies/current affairs they gave each of us a topic to prepare. We had to go to the camp library, read up the topic, write a report, deliver it to the group and lead a discussion. Topics given out included the Wolfenden Report, still topical at that time, Germany and its division after the war, the rôle of NATO, the rôle of the UN, the Middle East, Cyprus, Aden, Jewish/Arab conflicts, Malaya, the rise of Communism and of course the Cold War. Topic presentation stimulated our interest and drove us to the extensive collection of army pamphlets in the library. We also picked each other's brains and collaborated quite a bit and helped each other with ideas of how to present the topic.

We learned how to build up summaries on the blackboard. We learned about reinforcing learning by constantly coming back to it. We learned the art of question and answer. We learned about building up confidence in the learner, the use of humour, and above all avoiding giving the impression that we were in a school.

We put our skills into practice by presenting lessons to each other: quite a nerve-racking business when you have never done it before. And the rest of the group acted the part of learners asking difficult questions, pretending not to understand and so on. We found this immensely valuable, learning from our own lesson preparation and from the lessons the others prepared and presented and which we discussed afterwards.

Some good model lessons stand out even at this distance of time.

One entertaining lesson dealt with writing an accurate report, in this case on an evening's guard duty. The instructor collected random information about what had happened (mounting guard, allocation of duties and so on) and built up a random list. Then he asked us to sort out the list and put the items in a sensible order, and write our ordered list on paper. Discussion, with humour, followed, as various people read out their lists (many deliberately wrong). A 'correct' list was then written up on the blackboard. Everyone had to write up the report and one or two read them out and so on. He made the lesson very direct and very clear.

In due course we each presented our prepared topics. One man gave an excellent introduction to the Wolfenden Report, putting forward succinctly the essence of the report: e.g. the difference perceived between legal matters and moral matters, and the idea that an individual's view about moral issues was a private matter for him, and should not be a matter for the law. We all considered the recommendation that private homosexual acts between males over 21 should be made legal, a controversial area, especially in 1957, and the lively discussion continued for some time.

Most of us had scarcely ever spoken in public, so the skills required did not come easily. All Army instructors, however, whether instructing in the art of shooting a .303 rifle, or doing a smart right turn, or setting up a radio, or repairing a tank engine, have to perform before the men with confidence. Our course helped us with all of this and we learned skills useful in all walks of life.

They continually assessed us, and gave us written tests: passing out at the end was not automatic. We had to prove that we knew enough in theory and could do the job in practice.

One written and practical test that we all passed somewhere in the middle of our training involved film projection, working the projector, dealing with emergencies and repairing broken film.

'You will all be able to get jobs, when you're demobbed, working at your local cinema.'

I remembered the Saturday morning films of my boyhood, and the inevitable breakdown at the most exciting moment. It crossed my mind that in future, if a film snapped, I could rush up to the projectionist's room, waving my certificate, and insist on repairing it. The course took a whole day, a nice break from normal activities, conducted by the AKC (Army Kinema Corps). They introduced us to the Bell and Howell, and another more old fashioned boxy-looking projector whose name I have forgotten. Soon we could thread film like experts.

'Remember your loops; don't lose your loops,' still rings in my ears forty years on. We had to keep two large loops in the film or the thing would come unstuck.

'Where are your loops? Where are your loops?' He shouted as he went around.

'Could they be located in the hills?' we all thought!

'I seem to have lost them, sir.'

'Meanwhile, back at the ranch!' we all chorused sotto voce while the film instructor gave us a puzzled and pitying look.

* * *

We did more fatigues at Wilton Park than we had ever done at Fulwood. At Fulwood, we had cleaned our kit and our room. Now we found that we had to take turns to clean our ablutions block, swilling down the floor, polishing taps, cleaning sinks and lavatory bowls, and baths, and shower areas. Inspections paid much attention to the ablutions, and had to be spotless. We also had to help with washing up in the dining-room assisted by a huge dish-washer; it must have been twelve feet long. We piled the things in at one end, and it shook and rattled alarmingly, till they all came out clean at the other end. That strange-looking affair must surely now be in the RAEC Museum, but it did its work efficiently, and saved us many chores.

Guard duty however proved the worst of our duties. We dreaded it as a far more onerous guard than any we had done before, and as one that came up far too often. Straight after the evening meal, those on duty had to dress up in greatcoats and gloves, and head for the guard mounting parade at the main gate. After inspection by the orderly officer, the guard commander gave us our duties. One man had to be at the gate, with instructions to challenge anyone approaching. Hidden away out of sight, and after the IRA scare, armed with a rifle, sat another man, at a window, eyes glued to the gate; he watched the whole time.

A third man patrolled the extensive, well-wooded grounds of Wilton Park Camp. He carried a long, massive and lethal wooden truncheon. He possessed a torch, and a whistle. How well I remember patrolling those grounds alone, at dead of night when everyone was asleep. Every crack of a stick on the ground, or rustle of a nocturnal animal put my nerves on edge. I constantly turned around and shone my torch, to make sure no IRA intruder had crept up in the darkness. I always held my truncheon at the ready, as well as that whistle. As part of the patrol we had to enter the admin. block and inspect all the rooms; that too was a weird experience, one's footsteps echoing incredibly loudly through the deserted building. After the first hour the guard reported to the guardroom briefly, then set off again. We found this particular duty both lonely and intimidating, and rejoiced when after a few weeks, because of increasing alarm about the IRA, they doubled the guard, and we could patrol in pairs. The duty became almost pleasant when one had a bit of company, though it did mean many more duties for everyone. A nice consolation of this particular duty was that we regularly took a surreptitious glance at our records, filed away, unlocked, in one of the offices we had to walk through. We saw how we had done at Preston, and reviewed our progress at Beaconsfield, and everyone else's progress too. These records made very interesting reading.

Our return to the guardroom after the two hours became one of the great pleasures of life, just like the mug of tea and the food thoughtfully provided by the cookhouse. Then we luxuriated in those blissful hours before the next stint. We could lie down, fully clothed, and drift off to sleep, though fitful sleep at best. Every time I awoke I would pray the time was not yet up and drift off into sleep again. Of course it would all be ruined when inevitably, at some time in the night, the orderly officer and orderly sergeant called out the guard for inspection. Worst of all was that moment when the guard commander woke us up ten minutes or so before going on duty again, with just time for a mug of tea before going off for another two hour stretch.

Despite having little or no sleep, we had to do a normal day's work after guard duty. In the lecture room one soldier could often be seen nodding off after the awful duty, but no one ever took any notice: we had all suffered the same fate. I remember once, after a guard duty, taking some notes at a lecture and then when I looked them over that evening I found they were complete gibberish; as I took the notes I must have fallen in and out of sleep without realising it.

Throughout those nerve-racking guard duties, we lived in constant expectation of an IRA raid. To read the newspapers at the end of the 20th century, one could be forgiven for thinking that IRA activity started with the Provisionals and their violent campaign that began in the late 1960s. In fact the IRA had been ticking over for decades before that, and in 1957 they raided a camp in southern England and stole some arms. Our small isolated camp made an easy target, and they constantly warned us of the dangers of an attack.

Then one evening as we sat chatting in Hut 21, the alarm did sound. The place rose in uproar, with loud bangs and a good deal of smoke. We rushed to our appointed stations. We heard orders being shouted, and saw huge strangers with blackened faces round every corner.

Actually the IRA had not attacked. Something far more intimidating had happened: one of our crack regiments (Paras or Marine Commandos) had attacked the camp on one of their exercises. We did what we could, but they took the camp, and controlled it in minutes. I suppose the test for them was not whether or not they would take the camp, but rather how quickly, and how efficiently they would do it: well, they did it pretty quickly. It made for an interesting evening, and created some stimulating conversation for some days. The IRA itself never did attack. Perhaps their Intelligence had told them that there were men there trained by what the CSM called those 'regiments of the line' including the fighting East Lancashires!

* * *

We did no weapon training after Fulwood, but drill continued and soon it moved into a completely new direction.

The CSM began to concentrate on training us in the art of drilling a squad ourselves. But first we had to learn how to shout out and scream orders to the men. To practise this we were taken off to the football pitch, and with some men at one side, and some at the other we had to shout out drill orders such as 'Stand a-at EASE.'

We did not find this easy. We had to lose all inhibitions, and just belt it out full force. Eventually, we got the knack, and it occurred to me that we would have done Corporal Bowerbank proud had he been able to hear us. It also crossed my mind that the corporal at that very moment would have been screaming out such orders to our successors in Bhurtpore Platoon at Fulwood.

Once we had all lost our inhibitions by screaming across that football pitch, we began to practise, under CSM Stott's expert guidance, giving orders to the squad. The trick was to give the word of command, at exactly the right moment, that is, just when the correct foot was hitting the ground. To come to a halt when marching meant that the word of command, 'HALT', had to come just as the right foot hit the ground, HALT, LEFT, STOP! (or, 'HALT, ONE , TWO', as recruits would say). It could be quite tricky when the squad was marching away from you to give the order to halt, or about turn, and get the 'HALT', or 'TURN' on the correct foot; the trick was to lengthen the word 'Abo-u-u-t', till just the right moment and then bang in the order 'TURN' just as the correct foot hit the ground.

We never quite relived that exquisite moment in the cartoon where a trainee NCO, drilling a squad that is heading rapidly towards the edge of a cliff, stood there transfixed, unable for a moment to remember how to give the correct order for the men to about turn. The supervising CSM is screaming out: 'Well, say something, if it's only good-bye!' At many moments, however, when we forgot the word of command, or gave it on the wrong foot, the CSM certainly screamed out some choice curses when the inevitable errors were made, but as always, somehow, as in the cartoon, he did it with a nice sense of exasperated humour.

In time, as the weeks went by, to our own surprise, we became adept at giving out orders correctly, and took quite a lot of pleasure at drilling the squad, and watching it move smartly to our every command. It gave a sense of power, which I suppose we all enjoyed. Sometimes even the CSM would say, grudgingly, to some one who had drilled the squad brilliantly:

'Right, then, fall in!' This could be translated as: 'Excellent! You've passed!' We had begun our move upwards.

Inspections though made a constant reminder that we were

still in a training unit. On the whole we survived, but in the third week we ran into trouble. We had developed the habit of having a bite to eat in the hut in the evening, heating water on the stove, and keeping some food, cheese, bread, biscuits, in an unused locker at the end of the hut – a locker never inspected.

The inspection began in the usual way. We jumped to attention as the hut orderly saluted on our behalf, and then they buzzed around as usual. Then, as they reached the far end, away from the door we heard:

'Open that cupboard s'arnt major!'

There, in full view of all, we saw our half used packet of biscuits, some cheese, some bread. It looked so totally at odds with the whole army way of life that we all found it difficult not to laugh at the absurdity of it all, and had to make great efforts to look suitably chastised.

Lieutenant Colonel Hughes looked outraged and demanded an explanation, which he failed to get. The CSM went berserk, screaming and shouting about irresponsible, dirty, filthy habits. We clearly had committed a major crime. Our hut suffered no actual punishment however, but the CSM did not let us forget the incident for some time. We in turn, stubbornly maintained our habits of eating in the hut in the evening but took care to have nothing there at inspection time. We had learned the art of army survival.

We took a risk of course, but that paled into insignificance compared with those taken by one lad in C Company, John Curtiss, who lived in the hut adjoining ours. He liked sailing close to the wind, and this likeable character was always short of money, often without a pen and usually late. He had also lost lots of kit, and had never had it replaced: mess tin, gloves, that sort of thing. The inspection team always came round following the same route and, his hut being an early one on the rounds, he solved his problem by always borrowing the missing items from a mate in one of the huts to be visited later. After his particular hut had been safely inspected, he would slip out, unobserved, and return them to his friend's hut.

John lived dangerously, but he survived several inspections. Then inevitably, I suppose, about halfway through our time at

Wilton Park, the lieutenant colonel and his team decided to follow a new route. His friend's hut became the second one to be visited, and of course several items that should have been laid out on the bed were missing. We could see it all coming as we observed the retinue heading in a totally unexpected direction, and we waited for the explosion. We were not disappointed! The CSM's roar could, I am sure, have been heard on the A40 trunk road. He must have gone on for nearly five minutes. And the one who had been caught was the innocent party who had lent his kit out!

The miscreant owned up, but both suffered equally severe punishments with fatigues and duties and CB (confined to barracks).

Lectures and drill continued as key features of our training at Beaconsfield but PT too continued to be an important daily activity and it often got us out of the camp on cross-country runs, woods and escarpments all being within running distance, with plenty of streams to cross. We made the most of it, being unsupervised, and we would stop, or walk for a bit, and then make sure we ran in looking really whacked for the last bit. I do not suppose we fooled the PTIs, though at the time we thought we did.

On the whole we enjoyed PT but towards the end of our period at Beaconsfield we were taken through the woods to what they ominously called 'the rope course'. There before us, at a huge height, perhaps 60 feet, we saw a tight rope across a river slung between two tall trees. Two guide ropes had been tied on either side of the tight rope, about four feet above it. They told us to climb the rope ladder up the tree and set off across the tight rope.

'They can't be serious!' said someone.

But they were! I think we had all learned by that time, that you survived in the Army only by launching into anything you are asked to perform almost without thinking about it. You just got on with it. And we did just that. Across the rope we went without hesitation and no one fell to his death, which is what a fall would have meant.

We felt pleased, but glad that we only had to do it once.

Map-reading too allowed us to get out of the camp unsupervised and we loved the freedom of it.

We had been instructed carefully in reading OS maps and in the use of the compass. And eventually they risked they dropping us off in twos, in the middle of the countryside, urging us to negotiate our way to a rendezvous using map and compass. Somehow or other we always found our way, but we sensibly asked locals for a bit of help from time to time.

* * *

And so we lurched on, more or less surviving the military life, and getting ever closer to the time when our period at Beaconsfield would draw to a close. We trained to be instructors; we trained in drill; we trained in PT; we suffered all sorts of duties; but we also escaped completely from the military life for a few hours every weekend and this became very important to us. Indeed one of the great pleasures of Beaconsfield was the joy of getting out on a Saturday afternoon, especially when we learned how easy it was to hitch a lift. We would stand on the A40, in uniform of course (we were not allowed out without it), stick out a thumb, and although traffic was light then, within two or three minutes a car would stop.

One Saturday, three of us decided to hitch to Windsor, and within minutes a car drew up, driven by a middle-aged woman. She chatted about her sons who had been in the services, and her husband who had served in the RAF. Of course those were the days before the terrible increases in crime that have so marred the second half of the twentieth century. Those were the days when street crime was unknown, and nobody knew such a word as 'mugging'. Those were the days when a woman would stop and give three young men a lift.

Looking back it seems that the 1950s with its own particular charms and values actually carried on till 1963 and only came to an end when national service ended in that year. At the same time the Beatles had their great hits and a new age of freedom began which ushered in sexual freedom, drug abuse, crime, and a cult of the young. We also saw a cult of the casual. It became fashionable to make fun of the military and indeed anything in uniform. People 'marched' against the bomb rather than in regimental passing out parades.

Did all the change come about because national service ended?

It is more convincing to argue that national service itself ended partly because of all those new influences that had started to grow in the early 1960s, influences that had begun to turn people against the idea of conscription in peacetime. Those forces of change were those that usually follow great wars, but which had been delayed after World War II, and did not in fact take off till about 1963. Perhaps national service itself had helped delay the inevitable process, and the ending of conscription then released a lot of energy that needed to express itself.

Whatever the truth, we got out of camp whenever we could, and enjoyed lifts to all sorts of places, and people in the 1950s gladly stopped and offered us lifts. We not only got to Windsor, but also to Oxford, and closer to home admittedly, but none the less welcome, we got to High Wycombe.

We even went to London, but on our local train. The Commandant gave us all a day off for an important Twickenham match. We did not watch the rugby, but we did see London: the Tower (from the outside only) and Westminster, and Oxford Street, and above all we mastered the Underground. It was my first real visit to London, which certainly seemed to have some style at that time. For all of us from the north or Scotland these visits gave us a fascinating glimpse of another world.

Often on those weekends we left the camp just to walk in the countryside, an event that could bring its own surprises. One Sunday afternoon a group of us, following a route we had followed before, came out of a wood, and into a clearing, and there, about 300 yards ahead of us, we saw a large castle, as well preserved as Windsor, with round towers within its curtain wall, and turrets, and arrow slits, and battlements: a magnificent sight.

'Where did that come from? I don't remember seeing it last time we came along here.'

'We must have taken a wrong turning at that stile; we've come the wrong way.'

'No we haven't: I remember this clearing. The path continues over there doesn't it?'

We were completely baffled. Was this some sort of ghost castle? Some sort of mirage? We walked towards it. As we drew nearer it became more and more impressive.

'It looks really well preserved; people must live there. Are we trespassing?'

It was not until we were right up to its walls that we realised the truth. We ran round the back to check. The castle was not real at all. Behind the façade we saw the struts holding up a set. Beaconsfield film studios were nearby and this must be a set for a film. We went back and gazed at it in admiration, a work of art indeed that had completely fooled us.

'Where is the film crew?'

'They must be located in the hills,' came the inevitable reply.

* * *

The course at Wilton Park Camp lasted a mere eight weeks compared with the ten weeks of basic training at Fulwood. And, only three weeks after our move to Beaconsfield, Christmas arrived and we all got a short leave – except the Scots who got New Year off. That leave came just at the right time when we all needed a break from what had become a difficult and intensive course.

I returned to Beaconsfield for New Year, which I spent on guard duty, but that did not stop me calling in the hut just before midnight and seeing in 1958 with an illegal drink. We toasted amongst other things the health of the three Scots who were at home for Hogmanay. It was a significant New Year for us, and we reflected as people do on the past and the future. We had been in the Army four months; we had adapted to it; we formed part of it; it seemed the normal way of life. We had become well used to the Beaconsfield routine of lectures, cross-country runs, drill practice and trips into town. With the arrival of 1958 however we knew that we had turned a corner and the end of our training began to look very close: indeed we would be passing out at the end of January. Moreover we felt anxious to be off, looking forward to the end and often talking about it. We wanted to be doing a real job in a real unit even though we knew that this would mean that our close-knit group would split up at last.

'Do you think we'll get a home posting?'

'No such luck! Everybody here goes abroad.'

'I'd rather be abroad. And see something really interesting you know. I wouldn't mind Germany. You can still get home from there.'

'Yeah, everybody says it's a good posting.'

'We might end up in Hong Kong with the East Lancs!'

'Malaya more like, with the Loyals!'

'It'd be bit of luck if we all got sent to the same place!'

'No chance. Let's face it, we'll all be split up and sent to the four corners of the world.'

'I just want to get into a real unit, with less bull!'

'No such place. Being in the Army means bull.'

'No, I think it's different in a working unit, everybody says so.'

'Well, we'll soon know, it won't be long now.'

And so we moved inexorably towards the end of our time at Beaconsfield, working together, relaxing together, a very close group. We had of course made new friends: other soldiers from the other C Company huts, who had not been in Preston having done basic training in other infantry regiments. They spent all their working time with us, and we knew them pretty well. At night however, when not in the library mugging up some essential topic, we of the intake from Fulwood stayed in our own hut, cleaning kit, polishing boots, ironing things, snacking round the stove, and just chatting, but without radios, televisions, telephones. We seemed completely cut off, a group of young men thrown together and dependent upon each other. Fulwood had welded us together and we felt totally at ease with one another. We talked about everything: usually the events of the day, mimicking the CSM, or the officers, laughing at the system, complaining about the food. We talked about home: we all came from different towns. We talked about our universities and the courses we had followed and the terrible inadequacies of university teaching. Politics got an airing: the iniquities of the Conservative government, the follies of the previous Labour government. We talked about music, though we had no access to it at Beaconsfield. We made fun of each other and criticised each other with total frankness, and just enjoyed each other's company.

Then inevitably came our final week. Our time had come at last. We had passed all our tests. It was over. And it was time for the passing out parade. There was no military band on this occasion, but we did have the Commandant, Colonel Shean, resplendent with his full colonel's scarlet band around his hat, and the impressive red tabs. He inspected the troops after we had marched and performed our drill to perfection. He looked at everything, and then began to ask one or two men to raise their boots so that the studs could be checked, something they seemed to do at Beaconsfield though it had never been done at Fulwood. Either by luck or design, he stopped at the same lad who had borrowed kit and had got into such trouble with the Chief Instructor on that earlier Saturday morning inspection:

'Raise your left boot!' Then a scream of horror from the CSM.

'Where are those STUDS?'

'They must be missing, sir!'

('Meanwhile, back at the ranch!' thought I and without doubt the whole of Hut 21.)

Despite all that, which probably gave both the colonel and the CSM a lot of private amusement, we all passed out.

Shortly afterwards Part One Orders announced our promotion to the rank of sergeant. We sent off our battle dress to have the three tapes sewn on each arm, and we then had to whiten them, C Company style. B Company never bothered with such niceties but C Company prided itself on its bull. That proved quite a moment in our lives: we now enjoyed the same rank as the fearsome Sergeant Griffiths. We outranked the two corporals at Fulwood.

We could enter the sergeants' mess. We did pay the mess just one visit – and there was the CSM, leaning on the bar.

'Good evening, sir!'

'Mmph!' he growled.

We drank our beer, and then departed for the pub. It was too early for us to feel at home there. Nor did we yet feel like sergeants. We had yet to realise the power of the rank: it would open all sorts of doors, and make life so much more comfortable. And our pay would rise substantially, not to that of a regular sergeant of course, but even a national service sergeant received good money: certainly more than a junior lieutenant. And if sent abroad, as promised, we would qualify for an overseas allowance, and tax free booze and cigarettes: and all this after months of poverty.

We now awaited the postings. Where would each of us spend the next year and a half?

They posted up the information: destinations included Germany, Cyprus and Hong Kong but six of us, including me and another two who had served with me since Fulwood days, would be going to Tripoli in North Africa.

This was fantastic news. For the first 21 years of my life I had hardly been anywhere. My life had been exceedingly narrow, even allowing for three years at my northern university. But since being called up I had been in Preston, then in the south, I had met new friends, and had had unbelievable experiences which had altered already my whole outlook on life. Now I would be off to a new unit in North Africa. *And* I had two of my friends going with me. *And* we should be flying for the first time in our lives!

Wilton Park Camp. Made up to sergeant and ready for overseas posting: John Gibbons, Lawrence Laidlaw, Alan Kirkwood, Jim Gibbons, Peter Crawshaw, Dave Jeeves, Dave Brown, John Kelly. February 1958.

Like most people I had never wanted to do national service, but now I just could not believe my luck.

Things moved quickly. We had to hand in the greatcoat and gloves, and collect a fascinating array of new kit: three pairs of KD (khaki drill) shorts, plus hose tops, and puttees, three KD tunics, and a desert bush hat.

'What are the puttees for?' We all asked the question; none of us knew the answer.

Next came a mass of jabs, and a lecture from the MO about the dangers of too much sun.

Then came our last night together before splitting up. We got a little bit drunk and had a lot of laughs reminiscing about our five months together. We had become very close, and it was a touching moment when we had to part the following day. We optimistically exchanged addresses, but I think we all knew that, except for the ones who happened to be going to the same posting, we should probably never see each other again. And the rules insisted that we had to move on.

Yet even now, after more than 40 years, if I were to meet one of them, and go for a pint, I should be totally at ease in his company, such is the power of those remarkable five months.

* * *

4

Flying into the unknown

Our brief embarkation leave soon passed and as the time to depart drew near I became increasingly keen to get on with things and get away from home and indeed the UK itself. How refreshing it would be to do something different from all that 'training' that seemed to have occupied life up till then, at school, university and latterly in the forces.

Moreover, five months into national service, I was well and truly in the Army, and would remain in it for what then seemed to be a very long time ahead. Friends and family at home now inhabited a very different world and the friends and companions who mattered now were my national service comrades. It is never easy to inhabit two worlds and I think that all national servicemen when they returned home on leave felt some unease.

Going abroad would actually make things a lot easier; it would involve forgetting all about the old life and throwing oneself totally into the new, and going native. On returning home, one would re-adapt to civilian life, and move on from there. I did not of course work it all out then in such a precise way, but looking back I think that that probably sums up my instinctive feeling at the time.

We also felt genuine excitement at the thought of going abroad, a rarity in the 1950s, to a totally different country and culture, to what seemed an exotic place, a place of Arabs and Muslims and the desert.

Significantly, national servicemen had no choice in any of this. We did not have to concern ourselves about the wisdom or otherwise of any decisions because the decisions had been made for us. Most of us, if we had had any choice, would have acted sensibly and not done military service at all. We would have pursued our careers, avoiding that 'waste' of two valuable years, and the loss of two whole years of valuable contributions to occupational pension funds! But fortunately, in the 1950s we did not have that choice. For two years we just forgot about life's problems and all those exciting career possibilities. We postponed everything. We just concentrated on living entirely for the present.

So, no doubt with a certain amount of relief as well as expectation in our minds, we eventually found ourselves at a holding unit, ready for a brief stop-over, before catching the plane the following day for Tripoli.

It had been snowing, when we boarded the coach for Gatwick. At one point the coach got stuck, and we had to help dig it out wondering at times if we would ever get away. When we eventually saw the plane, a Viscount, it seemed quite small and lonely, standing out there on its own.

We climbed up to the door, and Dave Brown remarked: 'I'm afeart. What about you?'

'What?' I replied, puzzled by the Scots tongue at first.

'Afeart – afraid – are you not?'

'No,' I replied.

I had complete faith in all aircraft, and all pilots. Having been brought up on Biggles and his adventures, I felt confident that

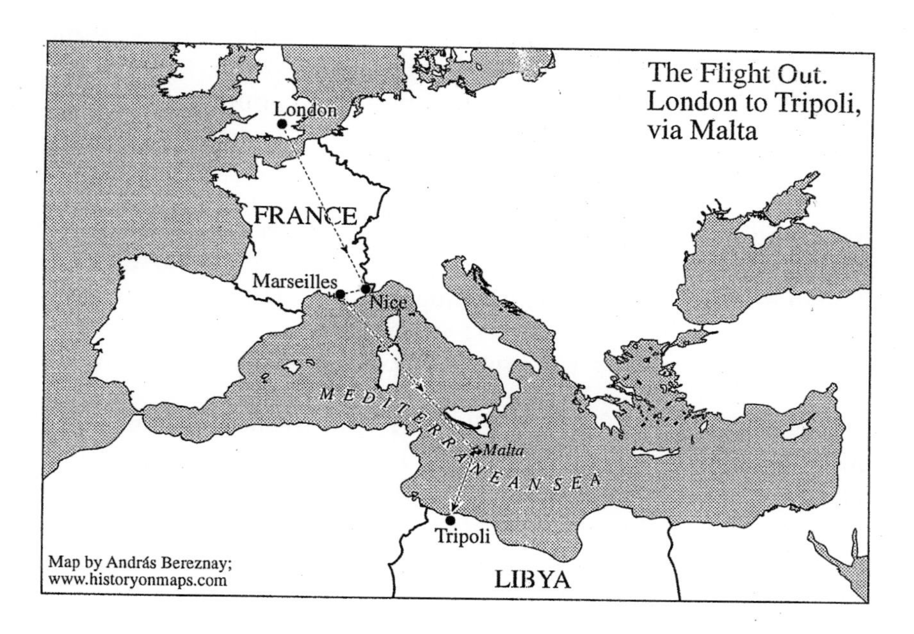

any plane could always get home if necessary on only one engine and with a fire in the tail. All pilots I felt sure could make fantastic landings in the most adverse of circumstances. Indeed, in my wartime childhood, planes had famously returned, night after night, 'on a wing and a prayer'.

As we settled into our comfortable seats, I looked curiously around me noticing the other young soldiers on the chartered Viscount. A number of young lads wore that well scrubbed, slightly worn and bewildered look of young recruits just out of basic training, now off to join their units just as our lads from Fulwood had gone off to join their battalion in Malaya. I observed soldiers from REME (Royal Electrical and Mechanical Engineers) and RAOC (Royal Army Ordnance Corps), and RASC (Royal Army Service Corps), all national servicemen probably, off to their first real postings, like us.

'Fasten your seat belts, please. Cigarettes out,' said an official sounding voice somewhere in the distance.

'Hold tight, we're off!' said the Scottish voice next to me.

The plane began to move away, slowly at first but gradually gathering speed. As we bowled along I expected it any moment to rise gracefully into the air but in fact it slowed down and came to a halt.

The plane waited there for a moment and appeared to quiver slightly as if deliberately holding itself back. The engines began to roar louder and louder reaching an unbelievable crescendo. Seconds later we began moving again but much more quickly this time, accelerating at an incredible rate, a rate totally unexpected and which took my breath away. No one spoke. The earth below began to tilt at an alarming angle and I realised with both surprise and relief that we were in the air.

'You may unfasten your seat belts, and you may smoke if you like.'

Shortly after that we started to eat and drink from our trays, and enjoy what seemed to me to be luxury travel! We had climbed up high and were in brilliant sunshine. White fluffy clouds lay just below us and the plane appeared to be completely still, suspended in space. In the background we could hear the faint and comforting hum of the propellers. All the while, the captain kept us well informed: we were flying over France and eventually we would land at Nice, our first stop, to refuel.

What a joy to be up there in that plane! It was like no other experience I had ever had. We all sat back and just enjoyed the sheer pleasure of it all.

After an hour or two, things began to change however, and the ride began to become just a little bumpy, ominously so.

'We are approaching Nice; we shall cross the coastline and then turn and approach the runway from the sea. Fasten your seat belts: we are running into some serious turbulence.'

The plane began to drop suddenly, rise sharply, rock from side to side, shudder alarmingly, and then drop again. People began to look distinctly strained, and I felt for the first time in my travelling life, very queasy.

'You look a bit green!'

'Do I? I feel it, too,' I replied.

The plane lost height and crossing the coastline it flew out to sea. Eventually it turned, dropping lower and lower towards the shore, skimming over the turbulent waves as it approached the runway, but instead of coming in to land, it rose unexpectedly in a steep climb and the earth fell away beneath us.

'No chance of getting down that time! Pretty bad conditions I'm afraid.' Clearly Biggles would require every ounce of his famous skill.

We all looked at each other as the plane came round in a wide arc making its way once more out to sea. It turned and in it came, skimming over those waves towards the runway. No one spoke and a degree of tension filled the cabin. Then again we climbed rapidly into the air as the earth and airport fell away for the second time.

And again the captain spoke: 'I will make just one more attempt but landing conditions down there are atrocious because of the weather. Make sure your seatbelts are secured tightly.'

We sat there, reflecting on the situation but saying nothing. I doubt if any of us had flown before and at that moment a single thought lingered in my mind and perhaps every mind on board: 'Is this normal? Is it like this every time you come in to land?'

'Always an exciting ride!' said a seemingly untroubled voice nearby.

Minutes later we skimmed above the waves for a third time towards that elusive runway at Nice airport. The windows of the plane dripped with wetness, either from rain or the sea. Who could say? Rough waves were clearly and alarmingly visible and seemed very close – too close – as we looked out. Then yet again we rose steeply and sharply upwards. Our pilot just could not, for some reason, land the plane at Nice.

'I am afraid it is impossible to land here. We shall fly to Marseilles, and refuel there.'

'Thank God for that!' said a voice next to me, echoing, I suspected, a thought in everybody's mind at that moment as the plane pressed on, most of us reflecting in silence on the excitements of trying to land at Nice.

The turbulence that had bothered us for quite a while began to ease as the plane made its way to Marseilles. No one had been sick, but I think most people must have felt poorly.

We landed at Marseilles without incident, thankful to be on firm ground, and enjoyed a look round the air terminal for a short while, before boarding the plane and heading south towards Malta. It had taken about three hours to get from London to Marseilles, and it would take a similar time to get to Malta. After another fairly bumpy flight well into the afternoon, the captain began to speak again.

'We shall be landing at Luqa Airport in five minutes. Because of bad weather however we shall not be flying on to Tripoli today. We shall stay over at Malta. You will be transported to Valletta where hotel accommodation will be arranged for the night.'

I think we all probably felt disappointed at not reaching Tripoli, a city that had aroused much curiosity. We could not wait to see Malta however, an island of which we knew absolutely nothing, and Valletta, wherever that was, and a hotel! And we had probably all had enough flying for one day.

We drove the few miles to Valletta. The hotel did not disappoint; it was a very grand place with a nice air of rather faded elegance. I pondered the Mediterranean Italian style, with its decorated balconies, chandeliers and the vast foyer. One could

Valletta in the 1950s. Grand Harbour, with the passenger wharf and (right) Floriana.

imagine that in the pre-war days the wealthy had visited and stayed in this hotel on their way perhaps to Athens or Cairo. To us it seemed a bit tired, as if it had not quite recovered after the War. They placed us two to a room, our room being huge, with a large balcony, and a very ornate telephone, which we would have loved to have used, but dared not.

We enjoyed some good food and drink in the hotel, and then set off to look at the impressive harbour, and walk down the famous Gut, a street of dubious bars each with its dancing girls who would willingly grant sexual favours for cash, or so we had been told. As soon as we entered one of the bars, several scantily clad, well made up girls, sauntered purposefully towards us, filling me with more than a little alarm!

'Eengleesh sargentee, Eengleesh sargentee, plentee marnee, plentee marnee!'

They totally misjudged our wealth! Unfortunately for them, and fortunately perhaps for us, these particular 'sargentee' did not have 'plentee marnee'. We had not been sergeants long enough to afford much more than a couple of beers each, which we ordered and enjoyed, laughing and joking with the girls, and after which we made our escape.

We followed all that excitement with a bit of a bar-crawl in the area of the Gut, and then, quite happy with our little stop at Malta and our first experience of life in the Army overseas, we made our way back to our hotel.

The following day we took off again for the last leg of our long flight and soon the plane began its long descent towards Idris Airport, south of Tripoli.

We landed in a large open bare airfield. I do not remember seeing any other planes. A few temporary shacks could be seen over on the left. Standing here and there, in ones and twos, were some Arab men with Lawrence of Arabia type robes well-wrapped around them, no doubt to keep themselves warm, because, to our complete amazement, it was snowing!

We found out later, that it was the first time it had snowed in Tripoli for a hundred years.

It had been quite a journey.

* * *

5

Sand, sunshine, and shorts

Tripoli's light snow rapidly changed to light rain and then stopped altogether. We did not feel particularly cold, despite the snow, the temperature being perhaps in the 40s. At the far end of the airfield near some rather rickety looking buildings, and near what I thought must be the exit, I could see some transport, a truck, and a couple of Land Rovers, and I rightly presumed that the different units in Tripolitania had arranged to pick up their own people. We made our way over there, and managed to identify our particular vehicle, which, like the others, had been painted in a pleasant sandy colour, very different from the dark green of army trucks back home. The young driver's belt and gaiters were of the same colour, fitting in well with the dusty airfield and the rocky scenery that surrounded us.

Soon we sped on our way, driving on the right-hand side of the road which felt strange but which, after a month or two, would seem absolutely normal. Stranger still was this first glimpse of North Africa. The dominant colour seemed to be light brown but we saw plenty of leafy evergreen trees and bushes and cacti and some very tall palms. As we learned later, this coastal belt enjoyed a Mediterranean climate with hot dry summers but mild rainy winters, allowing certain evergreen plants to flourish luxuriantly.

The brief ride was our first experience of that unique atmosphere of North Africa, something that would get right under our skin and almost into our very bones in time. It somehow involved all those light sandy colours and that pleasing, spicy, aromatic aroma that pervaded the air as we entered the outskirts of Tripoli itself. In time of course we would experience the great warmth and particular brightness of the incredible North African sun and the gentle nature of the people. It is hard to put into words that particular quintessence which is North Africa but those who have seen Libya will immediately understand what I mean. I know that if ever I returned to Tripoli, even after 40 years absence, I would feel it again the moment I stepped off the plane.

Mingled with these first impressions was that familiar sense of being excited and stimulated by what lay ahead. National service seemed to kindle that feeling all the time. The future always beckoned like an alluring mystery waiting to be uncovered. What would it be like living out my time, here in this fascinating country?

Before long, after negotiating the outskirts of Tripoli, the Land Rover drew up outside the gate of an army barracks and the driver began to give necessary details to the soldier on duty.

The metal double gates had a sort of see-through mesh, but in any case they were wide open and we could see a large parade square and some creamy-yellow buildings. The gates themselves were set in a tall archway above which was written: 'HQ

Azizia Barracks. Sentry at the gate.

Tripolitania District: Azizia Barracks'. On each side of the arch crests had been painted, each with a small sailing ship inscribed inside it; the driver had the same badge on his arm, just below the shoulder, the badge of Tripolitania District.

Azizia appeared warm and pleasant, with none of the grim greyness of Fulwood, nor that almost creepy silent rural feel of Wilton Park. Everything here had been constructed in that cheerful, creamy plaster reminiscent of those Spanish/Mexican haciendas we had all seen in John Wayne westerns. The word 'Mediterranean' sums up the character and style of the place for me, recalling pictures of Italy or Greece or Egypt. I remember the unmanned sentry box on either side of the gate, and beyond those, to the right and left, the two small pedestrian gates. The perimeter walls then stretched away with bits of vegetation, and Mediterranean shiny-leaved plants growing up against them. The walls themselves did not look particularly high: perhaps ten feet, the top half being a sort of plaster trellis work.

We drove in and saw, in full view, Azizia's large parade square. To the left rose large, tall barrack blocks two or three steps higher than the level of the square. I noticed a few staff cars, painted in the usual sandy colour, parked against the barrack block walls, and also a number of bicycles!

As we passed the guardroom on the right, we could see roadway-paths leading off from the square to other buildings in the distance. Here and there grew evergreen trees, and tall palms. Across the way, the Union Flag waved in the breeze.

Before I could take in any more of this fascinating and appealing new scene, we met WO1 Wilf Luffman, who, with Major Jefferies, ran the Education Centre, Tripolitania District, and soon we were being ushered into the sergeants' mess just to the right. Here we spoke briefly to Don Sinclair, a WO2 probably in his thirties, just out from UK, having arrived on an earlier and easier flight. A cheerful and burly national service education sergeant with a Welsh accent then came up, announcing with some triumph that he only had a couple of days to go. We learned that all other education sergeants whom we were replacing had already left.

Mr Luffman, a lively energetic man with a slight West Country burr, asked if we had had good flight in spite of the weather. He spoke rapidly: expected us yesterday; no harm done; see us all tomorrow at 68 AEC (Army Education Centre); transport arranged; get settled in that's the main thing; plenty of time; get a meal inside us; get some accommodation fixed. He told us that he lived with his family in married quarters but knew we'd like Azizia. And so on.

The WO1 gave the impression of being kindly, but no push-over, and extremely efficient. He seemed the sort of man who would want to get the best out of us, but who would look after his young sergeants and see they were not exploited. A WOl has the same rank as a regimental sergeant major, a rank that commands a lot of respect, not least amongst commissioned officers.

We soon chattered excitedly getting tips from those already there about getting something to eat and getting billeted.

Instructions seemed to be coming thick and fast.

'First get round to the camp tailor: you'll need to get the Tripolitania District badge on your BD and KD bush jackets straightaway. And three tapes on each sleeve of your shirts. We'll be in shirt-sleeve order soon; it soon warms up here once we get into March and soon after the instruction will go up to move into KD. And you'll need three tapes on your KD; we put them on both sleeves here. Sometimes you'll see them only on one but not in Tripolitania.'

There was a pause.

'And all your webbing must be blancoed into the local desert colour.'

Another pause followed.

I thought of the laborious hours we had spent during the last few months getting our webbing into its present pristine condition. Still in a way it would be rather nice to cast all that aside, put it into the past where it belonged, and start anew in what was going to be our permanent posting for the duration.

Then Taff spoke.

'Don't worry lads. Don't worry! I'll show you the ropes, before I get off to UK and demob – sorry to make you jealous! It's a doddle here. One of the Arabs will do your blancoing and your boots. They do everything here. Pay them something, not too much, a few ackers will do, piastres that is, the local currency, 100 to a Libyan pound, and they'll do a really good job for you. They'll clean your rooms, and clean your kit. They'll blanco everything in the local colour. They do all the dhobying – your KD has to be washed, starched and pressed just about every day. They'll do a first class job. Don't worry. You'll live like gents out here. No more bull for you. Hey c'mon, let's have a drink.'

What a lively character! He had worked with WO2 Lang in the District Library in town but both were leaving in a few days. Over a few drinks he gave us a lot of useful information about the set-up.

'Seriously I've really enjoyed myself out here. You will, you'll see. Any rugby players here then?' He had played a lot for the HQ team.

They gave us rooms, scattered around the camp, doubling up mostly. My room at the end of one of the large barrack rooms was spacious and square with two beds; the far bed had been made up, with a mosquito net over it. I found a couple of lockers a couple of chairs and a table. A large fan hung from the ceiling. My room-mate, a national service sergeant called Alan Goodson, an army reporter who travelled about getting news to send back home, was sleeping away, having been on an assignment somewhere or other, so I was alone for this first night.

I switched on the fan to see how it worked. I rather expected it to turn lazily like the ones I had seen in Humphrey Bogart's film *Casablanca,* but it whizzed round at a terrific rate causing a huge draught. I quickly switched it off; after all it was still only February, and quite cool now that night had fallen. I made up the nearer bed.

As I lay there my mind went over the events of the day. Dhobying! Arabs doing our kit. That gateway! Tripolitania District! Azizia Barracks! Those tall creamy barrack blocks. Mosquito nets! Those tall willowy palm trees. My home, my place of work, for a whole year and a half. Vague memories ran through my mind recalling all those films I had seen as a boy about outposts of the British Empire: films like *The Drum,* an adventure set in the North West Frontier of India with one of our great heroes, Sabu, acting the part of the Indian boy-prince helping the British troops fight off the raiders. Well, the North West Frontier could not exactly …

Then, within seconds, I fell asleep.

I woke early as we always did in the Army. Walking across to breakfast I looked around and again took in the distinctive feel of Azizia: those monumental barrack blocks dominated the scene. The one I had slept in stood on the left side as one came in through the main gate, one of four on that side, facing the square. I noticed that they had been well designed to keep out the heat. Three tall arches led on to a terrace, beyond which, protected from the sun, were the various rooms shared by corporals. The windows looked on to the sun-protected terrace. Beyond the corporals' rooms lay a long communal barrack room with windows that looked out to the side. I looked back at the block from which I had emerged; a window to the right belonged to the room I had slept in and would share with Alan Goodson. It looked straight onto the parade square facing the western sun but a ledge or sill that jutted out above the window would give some protection from the sun's burning rays. Viewed from the inside you would need to be ten feet tall to see out of that window. And it seemed very small considering the size of the room, but anything larger or lower would have let in too much sun and heat. Other barrack blocks stood opposite.

Everything felt completely different in appearance and atmosphere from anything I had experienced before and as I crossed the square I moved away from my John Wayne or my North West Frontier thoughts and decided we could well be in one of those desert forts from *Beau Geste,* the adventure tale of the French Foreign Legion popular in my boyhood. After all, the French Foreign Legion had been associated with North Africa.

The various sergeants and warrant officers nodded in a friendly fashion as I entered the dining-room in the mess. I thought them surprisingly few in number: a couple of WRAC (Women's Royal Army Corps) sergeants, a handful of youngish men in their twenties or thirties, one or two older ones, possibly with wives back home. Most members of the sergeants' mess at HQ lived in married quarters nearby. We would see them quite

Azizia Barracks. The mess, with Author (second from left), Alan Goodson (centre) and Don Sinclair (right).

often in the bar but not otherwise. I took my place at the long centre table and one of the Arabs employed in the mess attended to everything. That first meal of the day was a joy: steaming coffee pots sat on the table, and full English breakfast was available: porridge, bacon, eggs and so on. How different it all seemed from those cookhouses at Preston or Beaconsfield. For the first time in my army service that sense of eating rather primitively had gone and I visualised briefly those huge communal eating-places that had become the norm in my life; I saw myself queuing up for food with one of those utilitarian army trays. That had been our lot for five months but things had certainly changed since then. Then my Beaconsfield mates arrived and we compared notes about rooms and first impressions.

Afterwards, as we wandered back to our rooms, we noticed various soldiers attending the 7.30 a.m. parade and felt a little guilty. Early morning parades had been our lot since first joining up.

At 8.00 a.m. we sped through the barrack gates, and along dusty roads around the suburbs of Tripoli, again taking in that unique atmosphere so strong in that place. After ten minutes, we reached 68 AEC, a square detached building on the eastern edge of the town. The Army Education Centre looked after all educational provision in Tripolitania District. We went in and there, next to Mr Luffman, stood a tall, distinguished older officer, Major Frank Jefferies. He spoke kindly, introducing himself, speaking to each of us individually, and talking to us right from the start like colleagues rather than as officer to men. We grew to like him a lot. Eventually we sat down and waited expectantly to be introduced to the set-up and to what lay ahead of us for the next year and a half.

Brigadier Laing and his staff ruled Tripolitania District, administering it from HQ at Azizia Barracks. Major Arthur Downes, the SO2 (Staff Officer Grade 2, Education), whom we would probably meet some time, controlled all education within the District. We in turn at 68 AEC conducted the actual chalk-face educational work amongst the troops of the District, including the KRRC based in their own barracks not far from Azizia, and of course the soldiers based at HQ. Other units existed too in other parts of Tripoli, such as The Royal Signals and The Royal Engineers, and they also came into the centre for instruction.

The 6th Royal Tank Regiment however, though technically within Tripolitania District, lay 75 miles up the coast at Homs. They operated therefore independently of 68 AEC, and the education sergeants worked within the regiment and became indeed part of the regiment. Staff Sergeant McEwan was in charge there.

'We have decided to send Sergeant Brown up there to Homs to join the regiment. You will go there today, Sergeant Brown. They will send down their own transport to Azizia to pick you up. Look out for them. And of course we shall need a sergeant to work with WO2 Sinclair in the Army Library in the centre of town. Sergeant Kelly, we'd like you to undertake that rôle for the time being. Please report to Mr Sinclair, and arrange to go there tomorrow.'

Everyone else would work daily at the Centre.

He reminded us that, in Tripolitania District, all soldiers worked mornings only.

So Dave, a close friend since Preston days, would join the Tanks, 75 miles up the coast. I felt really sorry about that, but I supposed he might get down for occasional weekends. My job in the Tripolitania District Library right in the centre of town might be interesting; time would tell, but the job involved leaving with my fellow sergeants and spending time with a regular soldier, a WO2. Still we should all see each other after mid-day, when our work finished. And we all looked forward to working mornings only.

Afterwards we enjoyed a good look round the centre and its offices, and common room with the masses of materials for teaching. I noticed the current affairs information, and numerous maps. It seemed well equipped.

We spent the rest of the day sorting out kit, seeing the tailor and completing all the work that had to be done in that department. Then we could sort out those Arab helpers and fix up the webbing. And get a set of Number 3 dress, to wear at formal functions in the mess.

And then have a drink in the bar, and then see Dave Brown off on his journey up the coast.

'Och, one place is as good as another. I'll be all right up there.'

'Keep in touch!'

He climbed into the Austin Champ, a small open army vehicle rather like a superior American jeep, and drove off

I had lost an old friend, for the time being anyway, but that afternoon I met my new room-mate, Alan Goodson. We got on right from the start and having served in Tripoli a month or two he could, and did, offer a lot of practical help to us novices.

'Good to see you! You've settled in then. How are you doing? Have you got everything fixed? They told me someone would be moving in.'

The conversation moved on easily as I introduced myself, and chatted about the flight, and Beaconsfield.

'I'm from Bucks,' he replied in his pleasant vaguely south country voice, and then immediately went into a rural, Bernard

Miles, broad Buckinghamshire, which he called 'village talk'. Alan would often dip into this Bucks rural-speak for a bit of fun, just as he would often refer to people he liked as 'horse'.

He had worked as a trainee reporter in civvy life, and so the Army sensibly gave him a similar job during national service. I asked him if he liked it.

'Well, yes, I suppose so. I've gotta write some stuff up now. They bunged me into all this after basic training, and here I am. Yeah, it's pretty good. I like it. I've a photographer, John Perks, and we get out and about quite a bit you know. I have to sort of sell the Army back home, and send out good bits of news about what the lads are doing and all that. Hey now, what about you? You've found your bed. I always use the mosquito net though I haven't seen one of the beggars yet!'

'Nice room. I like the fan.'

'Oh yeah, the fan. Believe me, old horse, we'll need that when it heats up. It gets terrifically hot here, even at night. You'll need only a single sheet over you in high summer.'

I took to Alan immediately. His relaxed, comfortable way of talking somehow put me immediately at ease. And he seemed at ease with me. Sharing a room would not be a problem.

'Listen, just put your top-kit in the locker; you'll probably never use it again. No more inspections for us: they inspect the barrack block and the corporals' rooms, but not ours. Have you got everything sorted at the tailors? You'll need number 3 dress for mess functions. Talking of the mess, let's have a drink, so I can meet all these new arrivals.'

Work began in earnest the following day, and after breakfast I made my way to the staff car that would take Don and me into downtown Tripoli, where a number of administrative departments were located in the same building as the District Library. Major Shergold ran some sort of department to do with insurance I believe, and we would share his staff car. When the spacious Borgward Isabella drew up at the gate, Don and I sat ourselves in the back along with the major, who had been picked up at the officers' mess. Bob Lang, the WO2 whom Don was replacing, sat in the front. The engine gave a very sporty roar as it moved off and though I had never heard of the Borgward I liked its style.

That first trip to work gave me my first sight of the centre of Tripoli. I would become very familiar with the city as the months passed, but that first visit made a lasting impression. The car manoeuvred its way through dusty narrow streets where many poorer Arabs lived. But before long the suburbs known as Garden City appeared with apartment blocks and well appointed villas. Then we arrived in the centre, sweeping along boulevards lined with tall waving palms, and lovely white buildings.

This was by far the most beautiful and impressive city I had ever seen. I had experienced nothing in my short life that could even come even close to it. We overtook a number of swaying horse-drawn carriages, known as gharries, which apparently took you anywhere in Tripoli for only a few piastres. Then minutes later, not very far from the harbour and a distinctive hotel called the Waddan, we drew up outside an imposing though old fashioned building. I observed its shuttered windows in the Italian style and its attractive balconies with their decorated iron railings. Above the entrance of the smaller building next door I could read the words 'The Captain's Cabin'.

Major Shergold rapidly disappeared into his office but the rest of us climbed the stairs and entered the District Library which occupied the whole of the middle floor. As I glanced back I caught a glimpse of a young red-capped military policeman coming down from their establishment on the top floor.

The two WOs went into the library office to run over various documents and complete the hand-over process. Meanwhile I had an opportunity to look round on my own. The entrance had brought us straight into the middle of the library with its large central desk but I walked around the spacious areas to the right and left both of which contained generous supplies of books. I looked into the pleasant reading room that led off the right-hand section and sat in one of the comfortable armchairs, skimming through the magazines and newspapers that lay on a table. A lavatory led off the reading room and a balcony overlooked the street. A similar arrangement existed in the section to the left of the central desk but, in this case, the room with its lavatory and balcony formed the library office. Tripolitania District Library with its Italian feel and its high ceiling fans felt light, airy, and pleasant, and nothing like libraries at home. One could work in worse places.

At eleven o'clock, we all went down to 'The Captain's Cabin' for a break and a chat, joined by various army HQ administrators, and some civilians employed by the Army. We drank frothy cappuccino, served in a glass by the Italian who owned and ran the place.

Time slipped by, and before long we all drove back to Azizia, the first morning's work and an interesting experience over.

In the weeks and months ahead, I became familiar with just about every book in that library. I spent time re-arranging the stock into a more rational order and after a week or two if anyone wanted a book of a particular sort I could usually walk straight to it. Who would not enjoy working in that handsome building with its congenial company and constant stream of visitors? I certainly did.

And so after three days, I began to feel at home. We all lived at Azizia and I worked in the centre of a lovely and interesting city. I had many old friends from training days and a new room-mate whom we all liked. With Alan Goodson's help we made ourselves at home in the dining-room and the bar and right from the start a Pay Corps sergeant and a young RASC sergeant had approached us, bought us drinks, and started chatting as if we had known them for years. I think we all looked forward to enjoying the company of all these new friends, in the weeks and months to come.

* * *

We had arrived early in February during cold wet weather, but in March it began to warm up and the rain ceased. We saw no more rain till November. Up till that time my service seemed to have been spent trying to keep warm around a Preston open fire or a Beaconsfield stove. Now I learned to love the glorious Tripoli climate. It does not surprise me that the early civilisations of Greece, Rome and Egypt flourished, while their contemporaries in Northern Europe remained primitive. I put it all down the non-humid, pleasantly dry warmth of those lovely Mediterranean summers.

By March, we had changed into shirt-sleeve order, and very soon after that the order went up to move into KD. We had already had our KD dhobied and starched to perfection by the Libyans who worked at Azizia. It seemed a bit odd wearing a crisp, creased, bush jacket and shorts but, despite the starch, they felt comfortable and lightweight, unlike our heavy army shirts and BD. With just thin underwear we seemed to be wearing next to nothing. Our shorts, worn a few inches above the knee, felt pleasantly cool in the summer heat. Indeed when we first went into KD, and stepped out into the cool morning air of spring, it felt distinctly cold because the Tripoli spring usually stayed quite cool till the temperatures got up to the 70s by midday. But we soon got used to it. Eventually of course, in the high summer, with temperatures well into the 90s, it felt warm even in the early mornings and late evenings, and anything other than our summer uniform would have been uncomfortable: indeed, one sometimes saw middle-aged European males who worked for such organisations as the British Council wandering around in suits, mopping brows with large handkerchiefs, and looking very sweaty and unhappy. We, I am glad to say, never suffered in that way, though soldiers today in warm areas seem to lack our cool form of dress.

We found out at last about the mysterious puttees and their use. With shorts we wore long woollen hose tops (three quarter length stockings without any feet in them). They went on first, doubled over in regulation fashion a few inches below the knee. We then wrapped the long dark brown woollen puttees tightly round and round the ankle, like bandages, covering the bottom of the hose top and the top of the boot, and binding it all neatly together.

After 6 o'clock, long KD trousers replaced shorts for those remaining on duty. Otherwise, when off duty, even in the barracks, everyone wore casual civilian clothes.

The long summer that stretched before us, lasting well into October, came as an absolute delight, magical, unforgettable, one of the best in my life. It seemed to go on forever. The weather remained reliably warm day after day and I loved rising on those summer mornings. All work ended at 1 o'clock and then we could do as we liked.

Azizia Barracks. Author in summer uniform.

We could have had a siesta: but we national servicemen, and the younger regulars, did not believe in wasting the day like that, and we never did unless we had been up all night on guard duty. Our favourite excursion was to cycle to the beach at Piccola Capri which lay just west of the town.

'Only a couple of ackers to hire a bike from the camp,' said one of the young regulars. 'You've got to go. See you on the beach!'

We each took a towel and, wearing swimming shorts under our casual clothes, we set off. The ride itself took us through the sandy back streets of Tripoli. Poor families lived in small houses along little alleyways just off our slightly wider road, and little children occasionally darted out in front of us shouting and waving. Small groups of men could usually be seen on street corners brewing up strong tea over their little fires. We found it all absolutely fascinating, and I never tired of seeing this Libyan way of life, with its sweet smells and the occasional sound of distinctive Arab music that floated out of little shops or homes.

Tripoli is right on the Libyan coast. Indeed the city-centre fronts right onto the sea, but we were heading for an out-of-town beach: a beach which the Army seemed to own. We arrived, changed, and just lay there in the warm sun. We never used protective cream of any sort: none was available as far as I know. We started going to the beach well before the sun became seriously hot, and even then took care to cover up after a short while. Getting sunburned was a chargeable offence, and I never ever saw anyone with serious sunburn, or red peeling skin. Within a very short time we all looked quite brown and, once that happened, we lay in the sun with impunity and treated it with contempt. Our skin grew darker and darker but we never burned. Dark skin matching that of the Libyans seemed quite normal to us, and when occasionally a new boy just out from the UK appeared on the beach, looking sickly and unhealthily white, most soldiers could not resist calling out: 'Hey mate, get some time in! Get your knees brown!'

Climate surely affects personalities. The warmth certainly relaxed us and put us into a sunny mood as we laughed, joked, and chatted with each other. Sometimes we dozed off in the sun, feeling unbelievably comfortable and warm, almost as if drugged. Then we would race down to the sea and splash into the water.

As a child, I bathed in the North Sea, and people would call out: 'Come on in, it's lovely and warm,' but in reality, in my experience, the sea always remained near freezing. The water at

Piccola Capri however, really did feel warm, even at the first dip. We swam quite a bit under the blue clear water, eyes open, something I had never done before and we floated on our backs a lot just relaxing. We just enjoyed the water every day.

Only once did we take a risk, treating the Mediterranean with less than the respect it deserved. Lawrence Laidlaw, Dave Brown, John Curtiss and I decided to fool about a bit with one of those inflatable sun beds that could act as a raft. We pushed it out to sea and clinging to it for support swam out much farther than we should have done or had intended to do. Then as we splashed about and pulled at the raft, the lanyard and its stopper came undone and to our alarm the raft began to deflate. We were panic-stricken! None of us could swim particularly well, and without the raft to help us back to shore we'd have been sunk, literally. I remember John Curtiss clinging desperately to Lawrence who manfully struggled to put the stopper back in. He succeeded and then clinging to our semi-buoyant raft, we struggled fearfully for nearly thirty minutes to get to the shore against a strong undertow. We were quite shaken, and it taught us a few unforgettable lessons.

After all that excitement, we did as we always did after a dip, we ran back up the beach and lay outstretched in the sun to dry ourselves off.

When we grew thirsty, we would walk over that incredibly hot sand in our sand-shoes, as we from the north aptly called them, or plimsolls, or daps, as others called them: you could not bear your feet on that hot sand. We'd climb up some steps to the beach bar, using the sergeants' and WOs' section of course and order a John Collins, or a gin and tonic, or just a lemonade maybe, everything with loads of ice. There we would sit in luxury looking out to the blue sea and at everyone relaxing on the lovely white sandy beach below, and we'd chat, and joke, and just tell ourselves that this was no dream and it was going to go on for months.

That first day at Piccola Capri was very heaven, and we made hundreds of similar visits. Eventually, as the afternoon wore on, someone would say: 'Shall we get back?' And we'd ride our bikes back to Azizia. Once back, we would head for the cool dining-room where they served tea and sandwiches at 4.30, under the whirring fan: the perfect end to an afternoon on the beach. Afterwards we would go to our rooms, wash, shower, and change, ready for an evening in the mess maybe or a trip into town.

Day after day saw our group in casual dress cycling to that beach, marking out our patch and settling down for another afternoon in that long hot summer of 1958.

Many other folk used Piccola Capri of course and we often heard the cockney voices of young lads from the KRRC (King's Royal Rifle Corps). They cycled down regularly from their own barracks and splashed about with zest. Some older married soldiers also visited the beach with their wives and teenage children and many in our group, who wanted to find young girls of our own age, kept an optimistic look-out as we lay there sunbathing, but we had to reconcile ourselves to the fact that single, available girls were rare in Tripoli, so we just concentrated on enjoying ourselves and our own company in the sun.

At one point in the mid-summer, we did attract the attention of one girl in her late teens: a nursemaid, as she explained to us eventually, to a Captain Cobbold and his small children. We had spotted her, with her young charges, several days in succession and she had spotted us. Gradually we made contact and Olivia Brown became part of our group. A bit of a character, she enjoyed our company as we enjoyed hers. We invited her to one or two functions in the mess and she came, sat with us, and thoroughly enjoyed herself. Then she and the family moved on and we never her again. We missed her a lot.

Sometimes we would see an attractive teenage daughter on the beach with her family, and we would shoot glances in her direction and comments would be passed around about her relative merits, but protective fathers kept such girls at arm's length from us soldiers. In the 1950s the permissive society had not yet emerged.

We spent a great deal of time just lying there day after day, chatting and joking and endlessly quoting from Peter Eckersley's Flanders and Swann record, *At the drop of a hat,* with which, that summer, we became quite obsessed. John Heppenstall the young regular pay sergeant from Wakefield would start of us off singing the *Gnu song* or *Have some m'deira m'dear* and soon we all joined in the singing to much laughter. We loved the songs perhaps because making references to 'unperforated stamps' or 'beards in bed' came about as close as any of us ever got to sex in those days, so we made the most of it.

One day, on one of our visits to the beach as we lay in the sun after a swim, John Heppenstall, cried out in one of his hoarse whispers:

'Hey, look, over there; isn't that John Gregson?'

'Where? Where?'

'There!'

'Hey, yes, it is, it is!'

It was, too. The celebrated actor had come to North Africa to make the film *Sea of Sand*, with Richard Attenborough and Michael Craig. We already knew that another film company was making *Ice Cold in Alex* with Sheila Syms, John Mills, and Anthony Quayle, out in the desert near Homs where Dave Brown was serving with the 6th Royal Tanks. On one of his rare trips down he told us all about it. I saw that particular film some years later, and it regularly crops up these days on television and indeed is a fine movie, portraying Libya during the war when the Eighth Army battled it out against Erwin Rommel and the German Afrika Korps. The film has some excellent desert shots, and never fails to remind me of Libya. In one well known scene they have to get their heavy army ambulance (which they had borrowed from the 6th Tanks at Homs), up a steep sandy incline using the only way open to them: cranking it up backwards using the starting handle. With great effort in the burning heat, they eventually did get it to the top. In reality a half-track on the other side of the hill was towing it up, and if you look closely you can just spot the tow-rope half-buried in the sand.

Mostly, however, we did not see film stars, or do anything much except enjoy that fabulous Tripoli summer, bathing, dozing, and drinking cool drinks, but we held many a philosophical conversation on that beach too.

We used to rib John Heppenstall, George Finney and others for being regulars and asked them why they had signed on, and where it would lead them. They confessed that they would not be there forever, but it had been good while it lasted. 'There's nothing wrong with being a regular! I'm surprised you lot don't sign on. You've got a cushy number,' said George Finney, a young regular RASC sergeant. Doing three years certainly made a lot of sense because we all had to do two years anyway, and many young men, who would never normally have considered army life, did consider signing on for the extra year. After all, if you had to go through all the miseries of basic training anyway, why not make the most of the good bit that followed, and qualify for the better regulars' pay? Then, after a taste of the life, quite a few signed on for twelve years or even longer. But none of our group felt tempted.

Once someone said out of the blue, speaking with exaggerated deliberation: 'What – are – we – doing – here?'

'We're in the Army. D'you remember? Conscripts. Serving with the colours! Queen and Country.'

'I know that! But don't you ever think it's just unreal, like a dream, stuck out here, on this beach, in the forces. We should be waiting for the No. 19 bus and going to work in Leeds or wherever.'

We all knew what he meant. It summed up what most of us felt. Preston, Beaconsfield, now Tripoli, all seemed unbelievable somehow, especially this part, in North Africa. Would we wake up in a minute and find ourselves dozing on that No. 19 bus?

Sometimes we discussed whether the Army had changed us. We had to admit that in a very short time, at that particular moment in mid-summer, about ten months into our service, we had changed a lot. No longer civilians in any sense we had become just like the regulars; we were soldiers, serving abroad like them. We talked like regular soldiers: we knew their lingo. We mixed with regulars, and made friends with them, and had developed a contempt for all things civilian. To be honest, we had developed contempt for everyone in the UK including soldiers. At one point we heard about a heat wave in the UK, and someone had spotted a headline in one of the papers sent out to the mess:

> 'SIZZLING SEVENTIES : Guardsmen pass out on parade'
> 'Two guardsmen, standing to attention today, at Buckingham Palace, fainted in the burning heat, and fell flat on their faces.'

As we sat there, on that beach, with nothing on but swimming shorts, brown as Arabs, we poked fun at the whole idea of the 'sizzling seventies' and the pathetic weaknesses of those fainting guardsmen back in the old UK.

And so life continued, swimming, dozing, sunbathing, cold drinks, then the cycle ride back for tea, a shower, and an evening in the mess. Our summer was idyllic.

* * *

Of course we did not spend our whole time on that beach at Piccola Capri. We lived after all in a fascinating, large, Arab/Italian city, and we wanted to explore it. We ventured into Tripoli many times but the first time lives longest in the memory. One could get into town in three ways: one could walk, one could take a gharry (a horse-drawn cab where one could sit in the open and enjoy the air), or one could take the special army taxi, always available, which could be telephoned to bring one home. The gharry was cheap, especially if three or four people shared the fare. The taxi cost more, but proved useful at night, after dark, and quite reasonably priced if shared.

On our first visit to Tripoli centre, four of us took a gharry and carefully fixed the fare beforehand as we had been advised. Of course, as the months went by, and as we became old hands at the Tripoli game, we hailed gharries, and leapt into them, often recognising the driver anyway as an old friend and bravely argued about the fare later, but on that first occasion we naturally felt a bit more circumspect. We young soldiers loved to ride in such style: people today would spend a fortune on it, just to add character to an English wedding. We rode for a few piastre notes. They paid us weekly now of course in piastres, national service sergeants' pay plus an overseas allowance and we felt well off, with free food, lodging, and army clothes, cheap drink and cigarettes tax free and cheap. So we could afford to take a gharry, and buy a meal in town whenever we felt like it.

Our driver had said, 'Square? You want square?' On that very first visit, we did not know what 'square' meant, but we replied: 'Yes,' and we moved off.

The gharry swayed and lurched as it slowly trotted its way to town. High up, we had an excellent view of everything, and enjoyed seeing the little Libyan houses and alleyways with lots of children running about and plenty of men, but of course few or no women. The men as usual crouched in little clusters, chatting as they brewed their tea which they drank in small glasses. If not engaged in that, they stood still or sat still, gazing ahead, almost as if in a trance.

The centre of Tripoli always looked quite beautiful. It must be the finest town in the Mediterranean. It was then, and still is, unless it has changed, the most attractive city I know. We moved gently along fine wide streets lined with tall date palms, and alighted at 'the square'.

Immediately in front of us shimmered the blue Mediterranean, and Tripoli harbour. To our left the castle rose high, dominating the whole scene. Beyond the castle lay the old city: a place to explore at a later date. Tripoli's main streets radiated out from the square on the landward side and we stood there for a moment taking it all in: tall, grand, white-creamy buildings, fine streets colonnaded in the Italian style. Shar'a Umar al-Mukhtar (named after the Libyan freedom fighter) was particularly wide and impressive. We noticed Italian business people and shoppers and plenty of parked cars. Jaddat Istiqlal (Independence Avenue) led out from the square in another direction towards the elegant Roman Catholic Cathedral and the King's Palace. The former Italian governor's palace was indeed fit for a king, with arches, and colonnades, and domes. Palm trees stood in its grounds. Later we saw the palace lit up at night. The Corniche stretched away from the square along the fine sea front, in a curve, lined with trees and shrubs and with clumps of tall waving palms, and indeed much greenery.

On that first real visit, when we could wander around on foot, Tripoli made a great impression thanks to much Italian building early in the century. Libya had been an Italian colony and roads were still signposted in Italian as well as Arabic. Italian shops selling excellent clothes and jewellery mingled with restaurants and cafés selling glasses of Fanta soft drinks and local beer in small bottles, which we sampled every time. I recall fine gardens and ornamental lampposts.

On that first visit too we saw the very real poverty of the Libyan Arabs of the 1950s, before the oil boom of the following decade. More than once we heard the cry 'baksheesh' from beggars, one being a man with no legs, lying helplessly on the pavement, pitifully crying out as we passed. Here we first experienced the terrible conditions of what we now call the Third World. Libya remained very poor at that time, though the oil companies had begun prospecting. We all felt shocked and guilty about the poverty we found as the months went by. Why should Italy have helped itself to Libya and created an Italian town of grandeur while the native Libyans clearly stayed so poor? Why had those Arabs had to suffer so much because Italy and Britain waged war with each other, fighting in Libya? These questions crossed our minds and we often talked about them.

On that occasion, and on every other occasion that we walked through Tripoli, we saw another distressing sight: a man with a closed up eye, a horrible festered mess showing signs of serious infection and disease. Such men suffered eventual blindness in the bad eye. Trachoma, very common then, is caused by flies. Often one would see children with flies crawling over their faces and into their eyes. They did not seem to bother about it and never attempted to flick them away. Actually the flies in Tripoli usually would not move even if one did flick them away. In the evening when they buzzed about, or landed on the table, you almost had to pick them up to get rid of them. We all became obsessive about flies, knowing as we did that they would cause sickness and 'Tripoli trots' and we would not tolerate them anywhere, never using a glass if a fly had crawled on it.

I found everything strange and fascinating on that first day. As we walked on, absorbed by all that we saw, one of us suddenly called out:

'Hey, look at that, boys! Did you ever see that before?'

We looked, and saw two young Arab lads, about our age, walking hand in hand. It looked odd to our 1950s eyes but it turned out to be a common practice in Libya and eventually we became used to it and never commented about it again. It was another part of our education: the UK we learned was not after all the centre of the universe. Other cultures, other forms of dress, other customs, other ways: Libya had begun to teach us a lot.

Eventually we hired a gharry to take us back home to Azizia, and tea, and a drink in the mess, and a good evening talking about it all: empire, disease, suffering, poverty, differing cultures.

We regularly went into Tripoli after that first visit, usually in great heat because the long summer had begun, but we found that we could tolerate the heat, and it never kept us indoors.

One Sunday, two of us decided to go to mass in the great Roman Catholic cathedral, though neither of us was a Catholic. We took a gharry, and entered the great building, packed with worshippers. Tripoli at that time seemed almost as much a Catholic Italian city as it was a Muslim Arab city. At the far end, in the sanctuary, the priest was saying mass accompanied by several servers and assistants. We heard no word of the Latin service but near us Italian families chatted amongst themselves and ate oranges whilst the children ran around, chasing each other and generally making a great deal of noise. At significant moments a bell rang near the altar, and the people in the congregation would make a quick sign of the cross, and then carry on chatting. I came to the conclusion that Italian religion and culture was almost as foreign to me as Islam.

One hot afternoon, well into the summer, we decided that we really must visit the old city, down near the harbour, beyond the square and the castle. This proved the most fascinating experience of Libya. Without doubt, here within this walled city, the culture was Muslim and Arab and ancient, though we found the even more ancient arch of the Roman Emperor Marcus Aurelius. Narrow alleys funnelled all over the place, and we passed mosques and minarets, and traders selling all sorts of things in the attractive market called Suq al-Mushir. I bought a little brass dish, and a small Arab round hat which I still possess. We came across things like carpets which we either could not afford, or would not have been able to store. We strolled up 'Coppersmith's Lane' where the din of the hammering almost deafened us. Best of all was the Kasbah atmosphere of the place; we just liked wandering about. No significant numbers of tourists came to Libya in those days so it looked and felt like a genuine

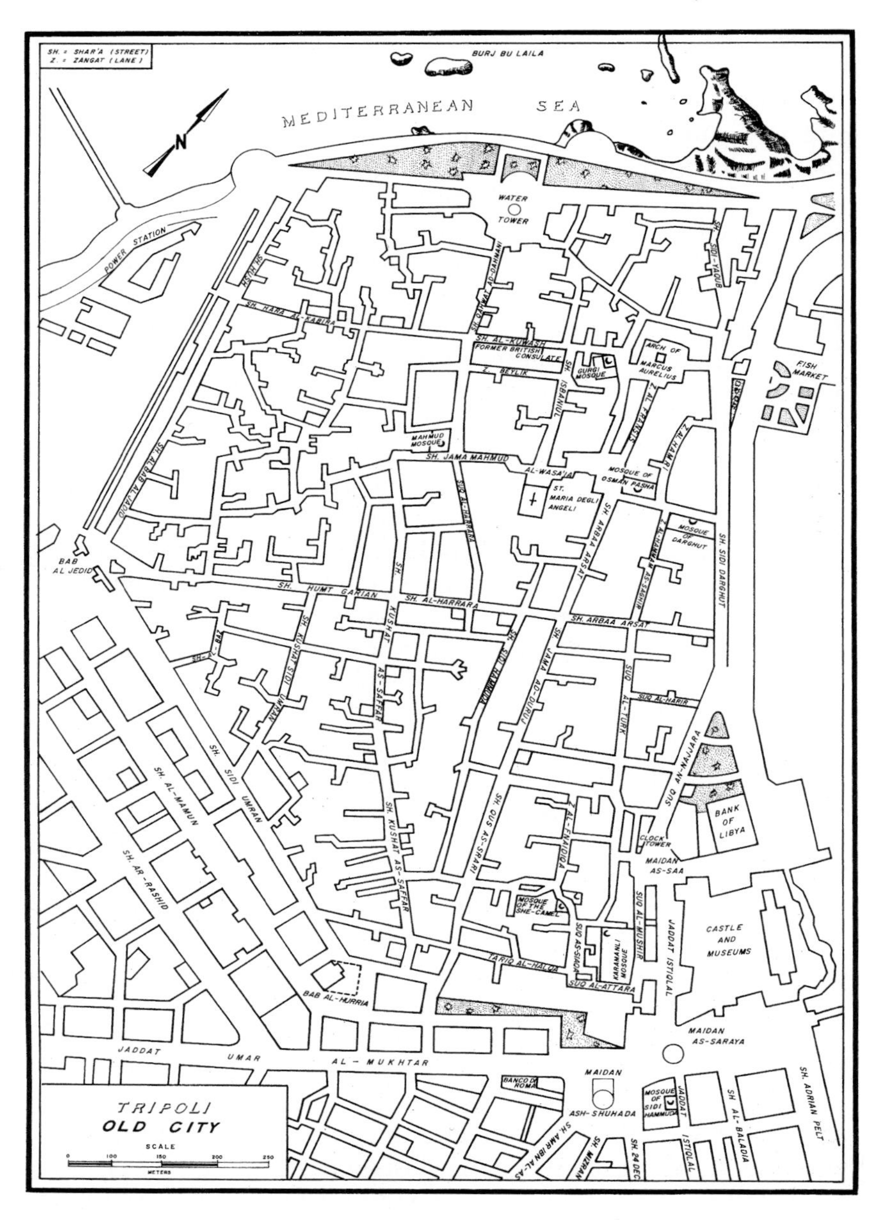

Map of Tripoli Old City in the 1950s.

Tripoli Old City. Suq al-Mushir in the 1950s.

place, not something manicured for visitors. If Tripoli itself was an Italian city, the old city felt Arab, as did the music in Tripoli and especially in that old city: it came from the Egyptian radio station which constantly pumped out anti-European propaganda, so they said, into the heads of the Libyan Arabs. That particular view derived from the British propaganda of the time: army circles abhorred Colonel Nasser, and Egypt, and the nationalisation of 'our' Suez Canal. The Suez débacle had taken place only two years earlier and because of that, 1958 was a very sensitive time for British troops to be in an Arab country. They warned us not to go out alone, but to keep in reasonably sizeable groups.

Sad to say, most British soldiers also seemed contemptuous of the Arabs, and always referred to them as 'wogs'.

'Get a wog to do it!' or 'The place was full of wogs' or 'These wogs are bone idle. They just use Ramadan as an excuse to do no work.'

I and my national service friends never liked such language or attitudes, but we were the exceptions. Most soldiers actually seemed quite fond of the Libyans in spite of the way they talked, and would often be seen around the camp chatting to them, and even photographing them or being photographed with them, so perhaps all that talk of 'wogs' and idleness was just verbal prejudice in most cases. After all, while on basic training we had been called worse things than 'wogs' and we always assumed that we should not take name-calling too seriously. Perhaps all soldiers, especially regulars, talked robustly.

On occasions we did normal shopping in the Italian shops. I managed to buy a nice Roamer watch at a reasonable price compared with prices in the UK, but generally we bought clothes. And those rare people with cameras always took their photographs to be developed at 'Photo Rapido' on Shar'a 24 December.

Sometimes we walked all the way along the promenade on the glorious sea front, afterwards dropping in somewhere for a beer or soft drink, though we found drinks in town expensive compared with prices we paid in the mess or at Piccola Capri. From time to time, we came down in the evening and went to the pictures. The Alhambra cinema sometimes showed British and American films and I can still see clearly in my mind's eye those huge Arabic subtitles at the bottom of the huge Cinemascope screen. We could also visit Tripoli's very expensive night-club. *Mokambo* in Shar'a Saidi, with its coloured lights on stage, fire-eaters, dancing girls, and the apt tune they always played: *Stranger in Paradise!*

When in the mood, we would go down to Tripoli in the evening for a meal at one of the approved Italian restaurants. The Army made it clear where we should eat and all cafés and restaurants were out of bounds unless they displayed the British Army sign of approval. I think none of us had previously tried Italian food, largely unknown in the UK at that time. We learned how to enjoy, and how to eat with spoon and fork, spaghetti bolognese, easily our favourite. But we also ate ravioli, and cannelloni, and lasagne. Also on our menu was fizzy acqua minerale, again something unknown in 1950s Britain, and red Italian wine which we really learned to appreciate with our meals. Again wine then was a rarity beyond the more well-to-do middle classes, and I and most of my friends had never drunk it.

On one such occasion, as we sat in a restaurant, we heard some American voices and they heard us. The middle-aged American couple, sitting right behind us, were the only tourists we ever saw in Tripoli. We got into pleasant conversation, and they showed great interest in us as servicemen from the UK. It did strike me that going on holiday to a place like Tripoli, or passing through on a whirlwind tour of the Mediterranean, might not have been a very satisfactory way of seeing the Arab world. We were enjoying Tripoli the best way, by living there, and absorbing its delights gradually. Meeting the Americans also reminded me of our incredible luck in experiencing all this at our government's expense.

We chatted to them about the American-owned Wheelus Field Airbase near Tripoli. Occasionally we met American airmen on the beach or in town, and would spend a bit of time with them. Wheelus Field greatly resembled a little piece of USA transported to a few acres of land east of Tripoli. They seemed to have absolutely everything in the way of comfort, and the American way of life ruled in all its abundance. We mentioned this to the couple: 'Well, we Americans love our home comforts. How's it for you guys? You don't have all these things?' We explained our life at Azizia, which they thought a bit rough. I thought then, and think now, that our way was more interesting. And after army life in the UK, Azizia certainly did not seem particularly 'rough' to us.

Often on those warm summer evenings we would walk home, as we did that night. We left the restaurant, and strolled slowly home to Azizia Barracks, past Arab houses with those aromatic smells of the east, and we could almost taste Tripoli's wonderful, evocative atmosphere. Britain seemed very far away that night: we might have been in Tripoli for a lifetime. Its ways had become our ways, its climate our climate: we were going native.

But we never got to the Waddan Hotel Casino. The well-known hotel, near the sea front, possessed a very distinctive tall white tower and had a certain appeal, but I think we felt a bit too puritanical, and too fond of our new-found wealth, to risk going there.

We did see King Idris though. Once, as we wandered along near the palace, a car with outriders sped out of its gates, and travelled off at high speed up the road and away. The King, a Sanusi from Eastern Libya (Cyrenaica), certainly lacked popularity in Tripoli, hence the speed, and the lack of interest in the event by everybody except us. My feeling was that most Tripoli Arabs disliked the King, the Italians, and even the British, but were prepared to put up with them, because they had little choice at that time. When the time was right, a group of rebel army officers got rid of the King, the Italians, and even the British, and travel to Libya became almost impossible for westerners.

* * *

6

We lived only for the present

We looked upon Azizia as our home and enjoyed returning there after a morning's work. Indeed we developed a warm affection for the place. The barracks lay on the southern outskirts of Tripoli, about three miles inland from the harbour and not far from the airport road. Azizia had once billeted Italian troops. More recently Azizia has achieved fame as the HQ and home of Libya's President Gaddafi and became a sad ruin after a notorious American bombing raid in 1986. In 1958, apart from being our home, it housed the British Army's HQ Tripolitania District.

Out of sight of the square and our living quarters stood the actual HQ building itself. Here Brigadier Laing and his team of staff officers and clerks administered ('managed' we would say forty years on) the whole army set-up in Libya. They too had living accommodation in the barracks except for those in married quarters, or 'the married pads' as everyone called them.

We who lived at Azizia were a very mixed bunch as was usually the case at any army HQ. If you glanced towards the gate you would see the provost sergeant, a kilted soldier from The Highland Light Infantry who, with his Regimental Police, manned the guardroom during the day, and looked after those men on 'jankers' (soldiers undergoing punishment). Another key figure, the RSM, had been recruited from one of the old cavalry regiments. We had a sergeant from the Oxford and Bucks Light Infantry and another from the Devons and Dorsets. The Army seconded officers and men from any number of regiments if HQ needed their services; some never returned. RASC (Royal Army Service Corps) people ran transport. We also had Pay Corps personnel and numerous men from the RAOC. I have no doubt that we all worked very effectively at our particular duties, but as a unit, as a group of people living at Azizia, we must have often looked a bit of a shambles, but an interesting and quite homely shambles for all that.

Our Camp Commandant, Major Mangles, a fine old soldier and a popular one, had been seconded to Azizia from one of the old regiments of the line. He had nothing to do with HQ itself as such; he and his orderly room ran the barracks. They organised guard duties, orderly officer duties, orderly sergeant duties, pay parades, the inspection of barrack rooms, food arrangements and so on.

At 7.30 a.m., after breakfast, the RSM conducted the inevitable morning parade. No one would have described it as the smartest parade in Tripoli: all those odds and ends from different places, however important their rôle at HQ, did not necessarily gel together as would men in one of the fighting regiments such as the KRRC. Fighting regiments had cohesion and pride, as we had seen in the East Lancashires at Fulwood. HQ could not aspire to anything like that. Sergeants avoided the parade as a rule, but every so often there would be a drive to improve things and the daily Part One Orders would instruct all sergeants to attend 'till further notice'. We would each then take charge of a small section on the square and generally join in the effort to smarten things up. On such occasions training by our old friend CSM Stott at Beaconsfield came into its own.

Fortunately this requirement never became a regular practice and mornings at Azizia remained on the whole quite relaxed. After breakfast we just sat around till the parade ended, though quite often someone had to dash off to the ablutions with 'Tripoli trots', a constant hazard for every soldier. We all suffered from 'the trots' – severe diarrhoea – that first summer though some immunity developed with time. Everyone blamed the numerous flies which seemed to get everywhere in Tripoli despite our best efforts to get rid of them. We learned to live with the affliction however; no-one ever went sick with it; we just put up with it. We drank fluids and avoided food for a short time and it usually got better after a day. Most hot places frequented by troops seemed to have had this problem, and one often heard from the regulars about 'Gippy tummy' (Egypt) and 'Delhi belly' (India), which seemed to be the same thing.

Then we all left for work till 1 o'clock and Azizia Barracks became silent and deserted except for a soldier standing listlessly at the gate, and perhaps a lone defaulter on 'jankers' lumbering round the square in full kit.

After mid-day and the end of work, Azizia took on a different character. A towel might be seen hanging out of a window. People might be seen wandering about in old shorts, stripped to the waist, or in various forms of very casual dress. Others like us would be seen cycling out through the gate looking even more casual with towels propped up on our handlebars.

Libyans employed by the Army would busy themselves around the place with cleaning and other duties. In return for being allowed by the Libyan Government to train our troops there, we gave quite a lot of employment to Libyan Arabs. As time passed, we gradually learned the background of our position in Libya, something which at first had puzzled us. The Italians had conquered Ottoman Libya in 1911, ending the Ottoman Turkish occupation which had lasted since 1551. Many Italians then settled there, and built up Tripoli as an Italian city with some fine Italian architecture. They also greatly ill-treated, and drove out from the fertile coastal strip, many indigenous Libyans who learned to hate them. During World War II, we had fought the Italians and Germans in the Libyan desert, eventually defeating them, but not before damaging Libya in the process and leaving land mines all over the place. After the War Libya was placed under British Military Administration but achieved independence in 1951 under the Cyrenaican Sanusi leader, King Idris. Two years later however, Britain had negotiated the right to train troops there, hence our presence throughout the 1950s. Oil prospecting had proved fruitless at that time, and the King found British revenues essential, but the British presence had another purpose. It served as a protection against the increasing threat of President Nasser of Egypt and growing Arab nationalism within Libya itself. Indeed the 1953 treaty stated that Libya and Britain would aid each other if threatened by any outside Power. Idris, as a Sanusi from the east of Libya, never felt secure in Tripolitania and he needed all the help he could get from Britain or indeed USA who also had a presence, and leased an airbase at Wheelus Field, near Tripoli.

The living quarters at Azizia included the NAAFI for the troops, a corporals' mess, the all-important sergeants' mess for warrant officers and sergeants, and of course the officers' mess. We younger people did not sleep in our mess, but some limited accommodation existed for the warrant officers and staff sergeants. The sergeants and the corporals had rooms at the ends of those huge barrack blocks.

We all enjoyed eating in the mess dining-room with Arab helpers waiting on us. Contributions to mess bills enabled us to have occasional tasty luxuries and we lingered over meals which became enjoyable social occasions. The two WRAC sergeants brightened things up quite a lot. We quickly learned to refer to them as WRAC personnel and certainly not as WRACKS. Everyone got on well with Sergeant O'Shea, enjoying her sense of fun and charming Irish brogue. She liked to 'mother' us a bit and tell us off from time to time but always with good humour. The other WRAC sergeant worked as PA (Personal Assistant) to the Brigadier no less, and kept us well informed on activities at HQ. An able woman with a sharp tongue, she seemed a bit formidable to us youngsters. Indeed, anybody who said anything that could be remotely interpreted as an insult of any sort to women lived to regret it if she happened to overhear it. I remember too the lively good spirits of the young regular sergeants: John Heppenstall and George Finney from the Pay Corps and RASC, with whom we relaxed everyday on the beach. And I must not omit the national service education sergeants, and of course, Alan Goodson.

A much older sergeant from the Royal Artillery, with a row of war medal ribbons, dominated the mess. Running it seemed to be his full-time job. He controlled mess staff, took charge of the bar, dining-room and kitchen and ran all functions and dances. He was a great character, a confident 'old soldier' who seemed to know everything about the Army and its ways. And if you were lucky, and in the bar at the right time, you would hear him give a great rendition of the old army song, *Bless 'em all,* in his fine gravelly voice. That of course would occur late in the evening when they had all had more than one or two. In the small mess bar at Azizia we saw the same faces again and again: a WO1 from RAOC and a sergeant from the same corps, a civilian, getting on in years, who worked for the Army and always drank Pimms No.1.

A middle-aged commissioned officer, Major Hicks (the quartermaster who preferred our mess) always propped up the bar at the far end. The RSM often looked in, as did our young lot, national service and regular, when we had not gone off into town or elsewhere. Whenever we called in. at lunchtime, or evening, they seemed to be there drinking and I think many of them stayed there the whole afternoon. Everybody took a turn serving behind the bar for what usually turned out to be a very interesting night. We remained sober, but watched everyone else slowly, or in some cases quickly, getting drunk, though the 'old sweats' seemed to drink enormous amounts of whisky without its having any effect whatsoever!

We younger ones tended to buy our drinks tax free and incredibly cheap and then sit outside. On such occasions we wore civilian clothes, with white shirts, sleeves rolled down and ties. We had brought out with us a few civilian clothes and, as our funds grew, we bought some good quality gear from an Italian shop in Tripoli.

Azizia Barracks. John Kelly (left) in the mess with Alan Goodson.

However, when we attended an important function like a ball, with wives and visitors present, we wore No. 3 dress. No. 3 dress, in white, was brass-buttoned right up to the neck, with badges of rank on the arm. The regulars, on such occasions, always wore mess dress purchased out of their own funds: the black tie, white jacket, cummerbund, and black trousers looked very smart indeed. The women wore evening gowns.

We enjoyed those evenings enormously. An army dance-band consisting of drums, piano, trumpet, and saxophone, blasted out the old tunes with a lot of noise and spirit. They played all the popular songs, for the quickstep, waltz, foxtrot, and also, 1950s fashion, the St Bernard's waltz, rumba, tango, samba, hokey cokey, barn dance, and of course, the military two-step. People who cannot remember the 1950s may not realise that these occasions differed completely from the BBC's stultified and formal *Come Dancing* programmes. Everything was rumbustious, with bits of jive, and much lively swinging around of partners, and even 'rocking around the clock' as made popular by Bill Haley and the Comets.

We did not dance much ourselves: we sat, and drank, and watched, slowly getting more and more drunk on our John Collinses, or Carlsbergs. I found it relaxing and pleasant sitting there, in the cool of the evening, drinking, chatting, enjoying the music, and also enjoying the buffet food when laid on. These mess evenings became a key part of our social life in Tripoli: something new for us, resulting from our promotion to the key rank of sergeant which had opened so many doors.

One of the big events of the year was the corporals' dance held in late summer, to which the sergeants' mess would be invited. We dressed ourselves up, and enjoyed a magnificent feast, buffet style. Again the older ones and their wives did the dancing. Most of the corporals, and we, largely bereft of female company, sat around at our tables, watching, chatting, and drinking, and generally having a good time.

On 30 August the sergeants' mess held its grand annual ball with food and drink flowing freely. I think we invited the officers' mess on that occasion, and people from other units in Tripoli. We probably invited the corporals too. This sort of social mix often took place in Tripoli, a little to my surprise because in UK I had felt that the different ranks kept themselves very much to themselves.

But life in Azizia had more about it than living it up in the mess. We enjoyed many quieter moments. After a morning's work, or after dinner before going to the bar, or perhaps just on any afternoon or evening, I delighted in going back to the room I shared with Alan Goodson, to sit, or lie on the bed perhaps, and talk about the day, or life back home, or people we knew.

One day Alan turned up with a brand-new wind-up gramophone, obtained from the stores. He had also managed to get one record and a pack of steel needles. We wound it up, inserted a needle and put the record on. We were both absolutely captivated by the joy of hearing Jussi Björling and Robert Merrill singing the duet 'In the depths of the temple' from Bizet's opera *The Pearl Fishers*.

We played that record every time we returned to our room. We never tired of it and played it over and over again. We liked too the other side of the record, another baritone-tenor piece from Puccini's *La Bohème*, but we preferred by far the sweet tones of the duet from *The Pearl Fishers*. Many pieces of music, such as Paul Anka's *Diana*, and *At the Drop of a Hat*, have special associations with my period of service, but the duet from *The Pearl Fishers* is the most evocative. We absolutely loved it, and wore out countless needles playing it. I just have to hear a few bars even now, on the radio, and I am back with young Alan Goodson, in that room we shared so happily at Azizia.

In the middle of the summer we heard some good news. A better room had become available and we could move in, if it suited us. It formed part of a modern detached six-room section, just off the square on the way to the HQ area. We liked it as soon as we saw it, with its lower ceiling and good decoration. The large low window with its pleasing view faced north so avoiding the hot sun. We began to take a bit of care, grabbing bits of furniture and a poster or two and soon made it a pleasant home to return to: with a special place for the gramophone of course, and our beloved record from *The Pearl Fishers*.

Alan and I became close friends during those summer months and, as we shared the same sense of humour, a lot of laughter emanated from our pleasant room. Often we strolled around the barracks, or up the road outside, where he would take a couple of photographs. Sometimes we just sat outside and passed the time of day.

One little diversion, namely baby-sitting, gave us a break from Azizia from time to time. Baby-sitting took us into real homes, though the 'babies' were actually older children, aged anything up to 16 years. Teachers from the Army school, when enjoying their active social life, liked to have 'baby-sitters' to look after their children. We came to know a number of these teachers quite well. They had made careers for themselves in army schools, which tended to be established in those days wherever the Army had a fairly permanent presence: places such as Hong Kong, Malta, Germany, Cyprus, and Tripoli.

They received better remuneration than teachers in the UK, and enjoyed excellent living accommodation in Garden City, with the right to attend the officers' mess. They lived in style, with servants for all domestic work. They seemed to live a life almost completely devoted to pleasure, but did not like to leave their youngsters at home alone. Hence a custom had developed of asking the national service education sergeants to baby-sit.

We always went in threes and fours. They would pick us up at the barracks after dinner, say at seven, and drive us to their very comfortable homes, where we could eat and drink as much as we wanted, and just relax. Though never paid anything, we liked doing it and it became a regular practice. I and one or two others regularly 'sat' for the headmaster of the Army school, Mr Eccleston, and his wife. He had a radiogram and numerous opera records which we played often, whilst consuming his Carlsberg and his gin. I remember enjoying old records such as Amelita Galli-Curci singing *Una voce poco fa* from Rossini's *The Barber of Seville,* and the same singer in the famous quartet from Verdi's *Rigoletto.* We loved this taste of luxury, living it up in their very comfortable home just for a while, and also enjoying an education in serious music. Eventually they would return quite merry, and we'd go back to Azizia, also quite merry, driven by Mr Eccleston though, if he was too much the worse for wear, he would ring for the Army taxi, and pay our fares. Then we'd go back to our room on one of those sultry warm evenings and maybe just put on that record from The *Pearl Fishers* one more time, before switching on the fan, fixing our mosquito nets and turning in.

* * *

Living in Azizia involved the usual round of duties. The barracks mounted its guard after 6 o'clock, with a sergeant rather than the usual corporal as guard commander. One guard had to stand by the gate, mill-board in hand, ready to take details of any vehicle seeking admittance. Another patrolled the grounds. Two hours on and four hours off remained the usual tour of duty. The guard wore the dress of the day, which for most of the year was KD. Long KD trousers became the rule after 6 o'clock, however, as it grew cooler in the evening, though in high summer we felt warm even at night. The guard commander would parade the guard outside the guardroom after checking names and bring them to attention at open order for inspection by the orderly officer, unusually one of the WO2s rather than a subaltern. Often it would be someone I knew from the mess like Don Sinclair, but sometimes it would be a little known WO2, one of the married men who hardly ever came to the mess except for the formal occasions when attendance was compulsory. Then we would all retire to the guardroom and duties would be allocated.

The guard commander got little sleep but I found the duty interesting, at least for the period up to midnight. A constant stream of people booked out and in. Eventually a number of soldiers would return late, fairly drunk and there would be a lot of good-humoured banter, obtaining names, and then packing them off to bed. The heavy hand of the UK training depôts never showed itself at Azizia. Of course on some occasions one, or perhaps two, or even three would return who were so drunk that, for their own safety and the peace of the camp, they had to be locked up. Braces/belt/laces and anything that might harm them had to be removed before they spent the night in a cell.

Quite often we looked after an ordinary prisoner too. During the day, defaulters trundled round the camp in full kit under the orders of the Regimental Police and did various fatigues before being confined to a cell during evening guard duty. And of course, every two hours we had to wake people up and change the guard. However, the duty, though a nuisance, never had that feeling of menace we had experienced in those woods around Wilton Park. We could also take a siesta the following afternoon and catch up on lost sleep.

Another duty, that of orderly sergeant, involved remaining in uniform and staying on call throughout the night. The orderly sergeant patrolled the camp, checking out the NAAFI, barrack rooms, and corporals' mess and making sure that good order and acceptable behaviour prevailed. Most people would describe the duty as inconvenient rather than onerous.

Going into the NAAFI and the barrack rooms reminded me what it was like to be without promotion and serving out time in the ranks. In the barrack room, national servicemen could usually be found lying on their beds or playing cards or writing letters home. They seemed comfortable enough, as we had been at Fulwood or Beaconsfield. The barrack rooms were very long at Azizia, in the Italian style I suppose. Long rows of beds lined each wall, facing each other across a floor that always seemed to have a covering of fine sand. Each man had a locker and plenty of space. They had to keep the place reasonably clean, display their top-kit in good condition for inspection, and get out on parade every morning at 7.30 after breakfast. Everyone wanted to talk when the orderly sergeant came on his rounds. After all we were not strangers to each other. We knew each other by sight if not by name and, although we education instructors had only just emerged from training, we quickly realised from the attitude of others that the strict regime of training establishments did not apply at Azizia, except when on parade, or guard, or military type duties. I also think that soldiers serving abroad had a different outlook from those in the UK. Somehow we felt closer to each other. These private soldiers, cooks, clerks, and signalmen had every afternoon off like us, and cycled down to the beach as we did. They also had Libyans doing their kit as we did. They benefitted from the overseas allowance and cheap fags and booze, and they too enjoyed the good life. There never seemed to be any trouble or any need for heavy discipline on those orderly sergeant rounds.

We expected guard duties and orderly sergeant duties but the Army always had a habit of taking one by surprise, even in a sleepy little posting like Azizia. While filing in the District Library one morning in high summer, Abdul drew my attention to an officer, a major, whom I vaguely recognised as working at HQ for the APTC (Army Physical Training Corps) and who, alarmingly, wanted to speak, not to Don, but to me.

'Ah, Sergeant Kelly, just the man I want to see.'

'Yes, sir?'

'The District Sports will be taking place soon, and I'm trying to get things sorted from our end at HQ. We've got all the usual field events. Should be a good day all round, lot of fun. Now I want you as part of the HQ team for the high jump. I'm getting people together for every event. I'm sorting out a bit of training for everybody. I'll post up the information of course but I'm trying to get round to everybody personally. Best way. So, see you at the training!'

'Yes, sir.'

'Well done.'

And off he went. I had long since learned that in the Army you just accept what comes and you never argue. That is what all the training had been about really: learning discipline and obedience.

I went into the office.

'What did he want?'

'Well, I guess I'm for the high jump, Don.'

'Why, what've you done?'

'Nothing, nothing at all. But I've been selected to represent District HQ in the high jump. At the Sports.'

'Didn't know you were an athlete.'

'I'm not. I didn't get a chance to refuse, or even to discuss it. You know the Army!'

"Never mind all that; I'm going to organise a cocktail party!"

Here was another surprise!

'Where?' I inquired doubtfully.

'Here, in the library" he said in his slight Aberdeen accent, 'for everyone who comes here for books, and their other halves: husbands, wives, officers, civilians, people upstairs, everybody.'

This sort of thing lay very much in Don's line. Don had served in London before being sent out to the far reaches of empire. He had enjoyed himself there, and often talked about people he knew and shows he went to: *Salad Days, Oklahoma!, Bless the Bride* and so on. That was his scene, wearing evening dress, and going to shows, rather than the military life, though he did sport the medal ribbon of the France and Germany Star, having just caught the end of the war.

He did plan the cocktail party, and everybody came, early one evening, and it proved a great success.

I worked with Don every morning and we saw him in the mess in the evenings, but not much otherwise. He certainly never came to the beach, but he did socialise a bit with older members of the mess, having the occasional meal in town, and so on.

Eventually, the big sports day took place on the field at Azizia: most of us took part in some event or other, though a few got away with nothing. We arrived already changed into sports kit, light shirt and shorts. The usual loudspeakers announced events, lots of visitors milled around, scoreboards gave out results, people sat around under huge umbrellas to keep off the sun, and refreshments were served in the carnival atmosphere. Every unit was represented. Dave Brown had arrived with the Homs contingent which included the 6th Royal Tanks' CO Lieutenant Colonel Vaux and his wife, Mrs Vaux, who was going to present the prizes.

All the usual events had been listed: long jump, triple jump, javelin and discus, and of course running at various distances, and the relay. I could enjoy nothing till my event had taken place; it would not do to miss it! I hunted around, and found our sand-pit. As I waited there for my turn to jump, trying to remember what they had taught me about the mysteries of the 'western roll', I could not help seeing the humour of it all. I had never been selected for anything, any event, any team, in my whole life. Yet here, in a most unlikely place, Tripoli, North Africa, I had to represent the Army Headquarters in the high jump!

It could have happened only in the Army which really had had a remarkable effect on my personality. I could now march, scream out orders, fire all sorts of weapons with accuracy, take

Azizia. The author at the sports day.

charge of a guard, do amazing things on ropes, and now, the high jump! The Army never gave up on anyone. No one could sit on the sidelines. You had to get on with it, and for a lot of people, including me, that worked wonders. We just had to do it and, amazingly, we did.

Alan Goodson, bless him, determined not to let my part in the proceedings pass unnoticed, waited with his photographer, ready to take pictures and write it all up.

'Look, John, I want a photograph of you, and I'll do a little article and send it home to your local paper. They love that sort of thing, and the Army likes people back home to see what fun we are all having.'

'OK!' I said.

The picture was duly taken and appeared with a few Goodson words in the local press.

HQ Tripolitania did not cover itself with much glory in the sports. The KRRC took most of the credit. We did win the high jump though, but not because of me. We won because the leader of our HQ team turned out to be the very major from the Army Physical Training Corps who had selected me, and who turned about to be an army high jump champion of many years standing. How could we lose?

Our summer physical exertions did not end with the Sports Day. At Preston, during basic training, we had achieved certain standards in physical fitness and passed tests. We never realised everyone under 35 repeated them annually. In late summer, Azizia Part One Orders informed us of this unwelcome fact and though things might not be applied too strenuously at Azizia, a tough route march had been placed right at the centre of our programme and had to be accomplished one hot afternoon carrying full kit.

It would be a strenuous march, but we had become pretty fit, cycling most days to the beach, swimming a lot, and often walking into town in the heat. A number of officers, certainly over the required age, had appeared out of the depths of the HQ to join in the route march, no doubt 'pour encourager les autres', and I think we probably felt encouraged by their gesture. We had no young subalterns at HQ, not being that sort of unit, so the older ones accepted the challenge of leading from the front. It helped us to accept more equably the sight of another middle-aged officer who decided to accompany us on horseback!

We found it pretty easy and, when the march was completed, we national servicemen looked comparatively unscathed by our efforts. Those older HQ captains and majors appeared absolutely done in, red-faced, and bathed in sweat. You had to admire them, and I think we thought quite highly of our Azizia officer comrades on that occasion.

* * *

Our mornings at the District Library in Tripoli I remember now with some affection. We had every type of visitor. Some officers managed to escape from their morning duties and visit us, especially those who worked in our building or elsewhere in town. We often saw teachers from the Army school and other civilian people who worked for the British Council or at the Embassy. Some readers worked for the oil companies. Wives came in and out frequently. Lance Corporal Parkin-Coates of the military police, a public schoolboy national serviceman, would also pop in, for a chat usually rather than for a book. We became quite good friends though I never ever saw him outside that building and had no idea which barracks he lived in. The SIB (Special Investigation Branch) people became regular visitors. The library buzzed all the morning long.

Our readers constantly ask me about books, especially fiction, and I had to polish up my acting skills to keep them happy.

'This is very good, moves very quickly. Lots of people are asking for it.'

'Really? I'll take it, sergeant. My husband will like it I think.'

'The *Darling Buds of May* was super. Have you anything else in that line?'

'Well, this is very popular – not quite like that but I think you'll find …'

'I think, he'll like this: *Boldness be my Friend*. It's about the war, and well written. Full of action. About a warrant officer who was captured by the Germans and tortured.'

'Oh well, if you say so, sergeant. I think you're right. You'll know better than me. Who wrote it?'

'Richard Pape. It's a true story.'

The library received new works of fiction and non-fiction regularly, every week, and we would set up displays and do all the paperwork involved in putting new books into our stock. One of the most popular books for male readers was by Otto Skorzeny, concerning his war exploits as a German commando: *Secret Missions: War Memoirs of the Most Dangerous Man in Europe.* It included a daring rescue of Mussolini. Another book, even more popular, was *The Darling Buds of May* by H.E. Bates. Everyone wanted that book! I listened to long accounts of how much everyone had been bowled over by it. It later became a popular TV series of course and I met the Larkin family for the first time then because I had never been tempted to read the book while in Tripoli; in fact I do not think I read a single book the whole time I spent there, though I dipped into a few, mainly on Tripoli and North Africa. It was as if I had done all my reading, enough to last a lifetime, at school and university. My new life involved living and doing and socialising, and enjoying myself, and reading played no part in it.

My work at the library was totally stress-free and happy-go-lucky with its constant trail of people, each one ready to talk. Indeed we became quite a social centre and one could and did set off for work in a totally relaxed frame of mind ready for a pleasant morning which passed quickly because of the constant succession of clients into our happy little world.

I loved being in the centre of town with a sense of really working in Tripoli, and I began to feel quite at home in that lively and beautiful town centre which I could observe from my balcony.

I spent my time doing bits of clerical work involved with running the library, and cataloguing, and keeping the books well arranged, as well as supervising our two Arab assistants Abdul and Bashir. Most of the issuing of books was done by Abdul, the older of the two, a man in his forties, intelligent and competent. Bashir was young, perhaps even younger than I. Abdul and Bashir looked after things totally when we went down to 'The Captain's Cabin' for morning coffee.

Getting to know these two Libyans became one of the most interesting aspects of working in that library. Bashir was a bit like the ship's boy in the TV cartoon *Captain Pugwash*, the boy who just smiled and said nothing. He was a willing worker who did whatever I asked; he cleared away books, carried books around, swept the floor. And he did it all with a cheery smile. He spoke only a little English.

Abdul never smiled but made occasional asides indicating a political agenda. As the weeks went by, we became relaxed with each other and he would begin to air political views which interested me. I knew little about the Arab/Israeli problem in the Middle East but I began to learn from Abdul, with increasing sympathy, the Arab point of view.

Abdul absolutely hated Jews; he would spit out the word with contempt. Nor were the British popular with Abdul, though he seemed to trust me and Don and treated us with some respect, asking curiously about my family and life in England. The British had taken control of Arab territory in Palestine after World War I, and had started inviting Jews to settle on land that was Arab, he said, neither British nor Jewish. Then the Israelis had been allowed to have their own state in 1948, created out of Arab Palestine. Israelis had murdered Palestinian Arabs and had driven them out after a successful war in 1948 and had made them miserable refugees. That was the 'Abdul version' anyway. All this of course had happened only ten years earlier and was clearly a recent event for Abdul. Then, only two years before my arrival in Tripoli, the British and French, allied with the hated Israelis, had attacked Egypt in the ill-fated Suez adventure. Abdul utterly condemned British action at Suez. I sympathised with Abdul here, having myself protested against it all as a student. Indeed, although I knew little really about the whole Arab/Israeli situation at that time, what little I did know had led me to sympathise with the Arabs. One must add though that the Israelis and the Zionists interpreted the situation in a very different way and forty years on the situation remains bitter and violent, with both sides convinced of the justice of their cause.

I understood too that Abdul, like most Libyans in Tripolitania, disliked King Idris who lived in despised splendour in the royal palace in Tripoli.

Abdul slowly and gradually explained Islam too, especially Ramadan and the need to fast from dawn till dusk during the Holy Month as one of the Five Pillars of Islam. Islam was very much in evidence in Tripoli. Slender minarets seemed to rise up everywhere, and the sound of the muezzin calling the faithful to prayer became part of our lives. We saw Libyans kneeling and praying in the street: they were a devout people. Few Muslims lived in Britain at that time – I had certainly never seen any – and all this intrigued me.

Abdul never mentioned his wife and family, and I never asked him about such things. Someone had said that it was not the right thing to do. You rarely saw Arab women in Tripoli. When in the streets they totally covered themselves from head to foot, with only one eye showing. It was very much a male society. Abdul himself always wore a small fez indoors as well as outdoors; Bashir wore a small round hat, the most common form of head-dress, with a long shirt and loose trousers. Many Arabs in the street wore the barrakan, like a toga wrapped around head and shoulders. I found it a little strange in a way to see only men and children in the streets.

Of course Tripoli was at that period still very much an Italian city with Italian architecture, Italian men and women, numerous Italian shops, and Italian restaurants. But after my conversations with Abdul I began to see the city in a new light, as an Arab place, but an Arab place which foreigners had controlled to the detriment of the indigenous people.

Those days in the library were very educational to me but, for the first time in my life, I acquired my education from listening and talking rather than from reading, as that long hot summer continued.

* * *

Abdul and Bashir taught me much about Libyans and their ways, but later in the summer an opportunity arose to learn even more. Major Frank Jefferies wanted to talk to us all at 68AEC. I knew him as a tall rangy man in his forties I suppose, a typical decent soldier of his generation. He occasionally called in at the library to see how things were going. He chatted easily to his young national service sergeants. He liked us I think and wanted to look after us. He felt bitter about Suez, which had taken place two years earlier and I remember him saying: 'Never took *The Observer* after that. Didn't back us up at all.' I, and most of my contemporaries did not share that particular view for we had opposed Suez politically, but we all liked the major, and I had developed some sympathy with the idea of needing always to 'back' our forces.

'Now I've got some news for you. It's time you all saw something of the desert. It would not do to go home having seen only Tripoli! You must get as much as you can out of your service. Right Mr Luffman?'

WO1 Luffman was the key man at 68AEC. He just about ran it, when not buzzing around in his VW people carrier.

'Right, sir,' he replied in his pleasant West Country tones.

The WO1 reminded us that we were all due leave, something which nobody ever seemed to bother about in Tripoli. He thought we should all tackle an expedition into the desert. He pointed to the map behind him, drawing out a route deep into the Sahara across towards Ghadames near the Tunisian border.

'Should take a week. Any questions?'

Everything became clear as our two leaders answered questions in turn.

'We'll take a truck and a Land Rover.'

'We'll have special rations. Easy to prepare and safe from flies.'

A pause followed.

'And we'll take spades. No lavatories out there so we'll use the desert and dig our own. And we'll sleep out of doors, under the stars. And we'll take compasses, and maps of course.'

We talked about little else for days. Alan Goodson wished he could be going, though he had actually been around quite a bit with his particular job. Don said that nothing would ever drag him on such an expedition. We by contrast could not wait to leave. It had come at just the right time: we enjoyed Piccola Capri, the mess and trips into Tripoli, but we needed a fresh stimulus before the long summer ended.

Soon we had left Tripoli behind us and we moved south across the Jafara Plain. The primitive road seemed little more than a

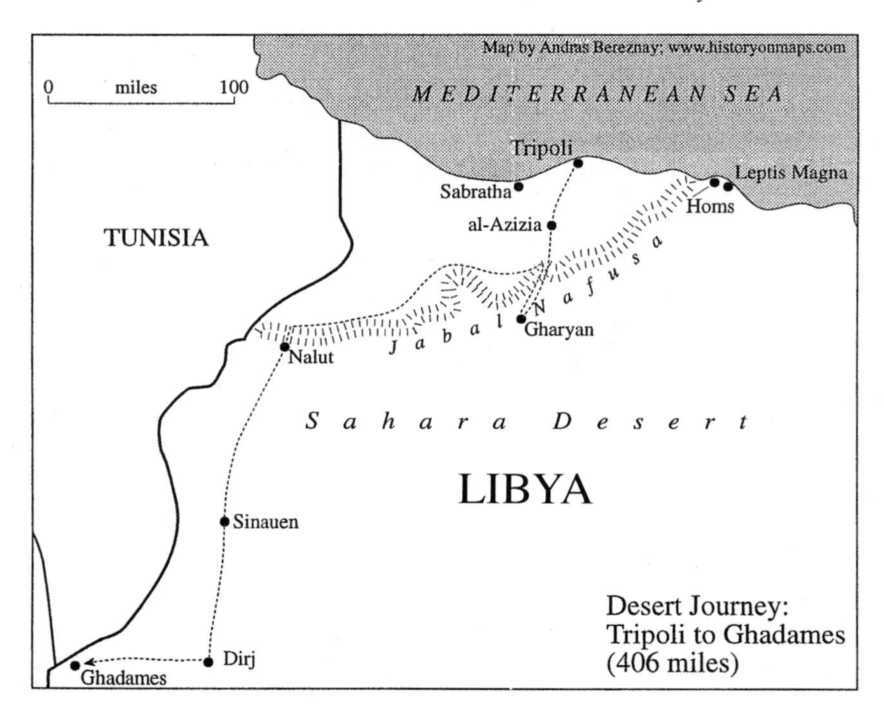

rough track in a vast, flat, stony wilderness. Every so often, hollows of loose sand would appear and we would almost, but not quite, get bogged down. Occasionally we stopped to stretch our legs and take the air, enjoying immensely the excitement of being in the desert. After a couple of hours we arrived at al-Azizia, about 60 miles to the south west of Tripoli. Temperatures must have been well into the 90s by then, so it hardly surprised us to learn that al-Azizia claimed the world record temperature of just over 136°F (recorded in 1922).

We enjoyed a break, and some food and drink, and then pressed on southwards, eventually crossing the Jabal Escarpment to the little town of Gharyan. The impressive winding pass up to Gharyan commands fine desert views, and Gharyan itself looked attractive and welcoming with its minarets and white buildings and trees.

Tighrinna, near Gharyan. Troglodyte dwellings.

However, the most interesting features on the plateau of Gharyan were the troglodyte caves, dug deep into the rocky earth, and home to the Berber troglodyte people. We approached one of the cave-homes and looked down; at the same time the troglodytes looked up at us. It is difficult to know what these people must have thought when they saw a group of strangers staring at them, but at the time we gave little thought to that. These caves had been dug deep in a very large depression, much too deep to get into from where we stood. They approached their homes by an underground corridor sloping down from the surface a little away off. The cave-home itself with its several rooms had been carved into the rocky side of the depression and could not be seen from above. Each hole or depression made a separate home, and there were a number of these at Tighrinna, this district of Gharyan. The cave-life was hundreds of years old, and we assumed that they had built their homes in this strange way as a protection from the extreme heat. These Berbers were a handsome people and their women, unlike the Arab women of Tripoli, were not totally covered so we could see their faces. We were absolutely agog with all this, finding it totally fascinating.

We also enjoyed a glance at the famous 'Lady of Gharyan' a large mural painted on a wall during the War by someone, from the British Eighth Army I believe. Her shape cleverly represented the North African coast

Back on the Jafara Plain, we stopped and watched the sun go down, always a moving sight in the desert. Darkness falls quickly there, with no twilight, and soon we wrapped up and lay on open ground outside our vehicles looking at the stars. I shall never forget those stars on that first cloudless night. They seemed terrifyingly bright. Looking at them felt almost like having a religious experience. I knew the main constellations and I picked them out easily and spotted what I assumed to be Jupiter. I had seen the majesty of the night sky before in my wartime childhood, walking home late with my parents in the blackout after late New Year's Eve celebrations and I was fortunate in having a childhood with none of the light pollution created by all those zealous vandals of the late twentieth century who insist on floodlighting every church and public building, and are doggedly determined to light up every main road they can find, even in the depths of our countryside. That desert sky however was uniquely different from anything I had seen before, stretching to the horizon in all directions. The brightness and the apparent proximity of the stars was awesome.

We spent the following days gently making our way towards Ghadames which lay far to the south west, some 407 miles from Tripoli. First we headed westward for over 100 miles along the Jafara Plain with the Jabal Ridge rising impressively to our left, till we eventually climbed up to the little hill town of Nalut. From Nalut we moved to the south for almost 100 miles to Sinauen, and then on even further south for 70 miles or so to Dirj. Finally we moved westward for another 60 miles to our ultimate goal, Ghadames.

As we moved to the south from Nalut, we seemed to be advancing farther and farther into the desert, with stretches of rippling sand amongst the stones and occasional sand dunes such as Europeans always associate with the Sahara. We stopped at a much needed well, raised from the ground level with a large pump on the top. Later we came across a spring surrounded by local people filling earthenware jars with water. We too needed water in that desert country and when we arrived at a likely settlement we always contacted the Head Man to find out where we could replenish our supplies.

The desert often surprised us. Once we came across a roadsweeper in a place completely devoid of inhabitants. He possessed several long-handled spades and appeared to be clearing the way and building up embankments of sand along the roadside, in the way that snow ploughs do with snow in colder climates. We passed an Arab boy standing by a sheikh's stone tomb; alongside it, several sticks had been planted with remnants of the sheikh's clothing fluttering in the breeze. Occasionally we passed donkeys carrying enormous loads, and once saw an Arab riding a donkey in great style, followed by his wife, on foot, some way behind. Near Sinauen we came across an old desert fort complete with battlements, a relic of conflicts long ago.

Within a few days we reached the pleasing town of Ghadames. The old city, built next to an oasis of course, had attractive white buildings and numerous palm trees and other vegetation. Its architecture interested us, in that it had been cleverly designed to keep out the sun. It had shady covered ways, and the place remained remarkably cool, in spite of the intense dry heat of the summer. Women used the house roofs and walkways to get around while men walked at ground level. The whole place had a remote, peaceful air about it and I could have happily stayed there for days.

After Ghadames, we continued our journey heading homewards, but visiting little settlements from time to time and enjoying sightings of scorpions and other interesting creatures. We also encountered camels and bedu, and even occasional groups of Tuaregs. The people always treated us in a friendly manner. We trundled into one oasis in particular with a large inviting stretch of water and plenty of trees, and crowds of children ran forward as usual to greet us calling 'baksheesh, baksheesh'. We stayed a while at that welcoming place and

Ghadames. A winding street in the old oasis.

enjoyed the hospitality of the desert people and filled up again with water. During our time in Libya we had all got into the habit of actually using lots of Arabic words: shahi (tea), kwayyis (yes, all right), min fadlak (please), shukran (thank you), imshi (go away!), bint (woman), shufti (look) but none of us could converse in Arabic, except, to our amazement, our main driver and we made full use of his skills when we called in at remote oases.

The whole magnificent journey allowed us to appreciate the vastness of Libya and the Libyan desert though actually we had only seen a tiny bit of the north west corner. Eventually though, as the days passed, we began to look forward to returning home to Azizia and the bar and one of those ice-cold Carlsbergs we enjoyed so much.

Before we reached the civilised environs of Tripoli, however, we did experience one severe sandstorm, locally known as a ghibli. We had curled up for the night as usual, on the ground. Then I remember wakening to a terrific wind blowing everywhere. I wrapped the blanket around me as well as I could, and drifted in and out of sleep, but on waking again, I could scarcely open my eyes now horribly caked with sand. I could just make out the others as they staggered around in a similar condition. We made our way to our vehicle, and what we hoped might be some shelter from the ferocious wind. Inside however we could see nothing but masses of flies crawling in all directions like a scene from a science fiction film. They covered every surface and we retreated in haste and horror. Eventually the wind died down and we cleaned ourselves up, got rid of the flies with some difficulty, and set off once again.

After that sandstorm Tripoli seemed more and more inviting; the desert had been fascinating, and gave us plenty to talk about on the beach with our friends, but we returned home to Azizia Barracks with real joy.

Not long after our return, 68 AEC managed to fit in another visit: a brief one to the Roman site at Sabratha, about an hour's drive on the other side of Piccola Capri. In early times, three cities could be found in our part of North Africa: Tripoli or Oea in the centre, Leptis Magna to the east, and Sabratha to the west.

Roman Sabratha dated from the first and second centuries AD, but the Byzantine Emperor Justinian added much in the 6th century. The magnificent theatre dominated, but much else aroused interest such as the baths and temples and above all the atmosphere of antiquity that surrounded the place.

Apart from such excursions life carried on as usual: a morning's work, an afternoon's pleasure usually on the beach or in town, and an evening in the mess. Apart from the occasional guard duty, military matters did not usually enter our easy existence.

The real army and real parades had really impressed us though when the KRRC, the 60th Rifles, gave a brilliant Queen's Birthday Parade at Azizia. We watched in admiration as they came onto the square, very smart in KD shorts, bush jackets, boots, puttees, hose tops, and green berets. They marched at their incredibly fast light infantry rate, all to the unique sound of their

KRRC Queen's Birthday Parade at Azizia Barracks, 1958.

bugle band and drums. It sounded and looked terrific: bugles blasting, the riflemen almost running. We heard a 21-gun salute at the same time as the riflemen gave a magnificent 'feu de joie'. Such regiments beat the Guards any time, I believe, for smartness, speed and sheer spectacle. Our Commander, Brigadier G. Laing CBE, and the British Ambassador took the Salute.

As autumn approached we felt sad because KRRC would depart soon. We had seen quite a lot of them in one way or another. I remember thinking that soon they would all board a troopship and Gialo barracks would lie empty, for things were moving on. In a year it would be our turn, a strange thought. The Army had become an impelling way of life, and Libya had exercised such a magnetic grip, it seemed inconceivable somehow that it would all end and mundane civilian life would take over once again. Still, we had a long way to go: we were only just approaching the halfway point. The Royal Irish Fusiliers we heard would be out soon to replace the KRRC.

* * *

Our desert excursion marked the last days of summer. It had just gone on and on and even in September it remained hot and we continued to go to the beach, lying in the sun, chatting.

'Hey, we ought to do something.'

'No, thanks.'

'No, I mean it's our anniversary. We've been in the Army a year nearly. September 12th.'

'Yeah, he's right: one year down, one to go. Two years seemed endless. Do you remember?'

'Still does. It seems a lifetime since we came in.'

We decided we should go into town for spaghetti and wine. I sensed that at that time, late summer in Tripoli, cut off from the world we had known, we had a feeling of contentment. Each of our long days seemed like three: morning at work; afternoon on the beach or whatever; evening in the mess or out and about. We had none of that desperate longing for the weekend so much in evidence during training. Each day passed without stress. We just drifted along, always in good company, with good food, good drink, and good weather. We lived purely for the present; the future could take care of itself.

The immediate future was the end of summer which came to Tripoli in October, and as the weather cooled we discarded KD. It began to feel cold to us, but in fact temperatures remained in the low 60s. Remembrance Day approached, of course, and would be marked by a special service in the Garrison Church, a fine spacious modern building near the barracks.

Everyone attended the moving service. After a sermon, the Last Post, and Reveille, we sang that best of all Remembrance Day hymns, 'O valiant hearts.'

The haunting tune and moving words had a profound effect on me then and still have now.

I knew that many there that day had fought in the War, and had seen comrades die. I knew of national servicemen serving at that moment, and dying, in Malaya and Cyprus. Cyprus felt close to us, as part of Middle East Command. Indeed we saw people who moved regularly between Cyprus and Tripoli and who brought disturbing tales to us in the mess. Fighting had also taken place at Suez only two years earlier, and though I had been against it politically there could be no criticism of the armed forces who did their duty as they always had done.

Having been to such a Remembrance Service as that one in Tripoli, I was horrified in later years when some clever young things went about with white poppies for peace, and tried to suggest that those who mourned their dead with red poppies were warmongers. I have never met any group who hated war more than those soldiers who had experienced its horrors. Many attended that service on that Remembrance Day in Tripoli in 1958.

In cool December, we appreciated the benefit of wearing full BD again, especially when on guard duty. I looked forward to a Tripoli Christmas, and the festivities planned for the mess. I felt really settled in Tripoli, with plenty of friends, a pleasing routine, and another glorious Tripoli summer to look forward to, and then a flight home, and the end of my service. The Army though, as so often, came up with the totally unexpected.

Only a week before Christmas, as I was settling down to some work in the District Library, Don emerged from the office:

'HQ's been on the phone. The SO2 wants to see you, John.'

'The SO2? Why?'

'No idea. Captain Beech is coming down here, on business with somebody downstairs apparently, at about 10.00; Major Downes has arranged for you to have a lift back to HQ with him.'

I felt puzzled and slightly alarmed. The SO2, our boss and our staff officer at HQ, had the reputation of a stickler, and none of us had so much as spoken to him up till now. At just after ten, the captain burst in; he was a bluff cheerful man whom I had come across before.

'Ready, sergeant? Let's be off. I understand you've been summoned from on high?'

'Yes, sir, the SO2.'

'Good luck!'

We drove off quickly. One of those swift but skilful drivers, he swerved here and lurched there on our way back to Azizia, chatting away merrily all the while. At one point, when a young boy raced right across our path as children often did, the captain swerved brilliantly and the boy, by some miracle, managed to escape unscathed.

'Damn! Missed him!' shouted the captain, and we raced on, finally reaching the barracks, in spite of everything, in one piece.

I entered the HQ building for the first time in my life, found the correct door, knocked, entered, came to attention, and saluted.

The SO2 asked me to sit and began asking questions about my work. I talked about my mornings at the District Library, and the various tasks I performed, and how I would nevertheless have enjoyed doing some instructing. During a pause I began to wonder what all this might be leading to. The SO2 looked at me directly and said he was glad to hear all that but had to inform me that he had called me for a talk because Mr Sinclair had indicated dissatisfaction with my work.

I could scarcely believe this, because Don had never uttered a word of criticism about anything I had ever done. I felt utterly shocked, but I remember well my cool reply.

'I am surprised to hear that,' I said. 'If Mr Sinclair is not satisfied with my work, then why has he not said so to me?'

I received no satisfactory response but the SO2 went on to say that he wanted me to move from the library with immediate effect. He had decided to send me to the 6th Royal Tanks at Homs to replace Dave Brown who would come to Tripoli. I said nothing but thought that it would be good to do some instructing; after all, that is what I had been trained to do.

He then went to fill in the details of the moves. All this would all happen straight after Christmas, only a few days away, and Dave Brown would spend Christmas up at Homs before coming to Tripoli. However, I must pack up immediately, leave Azizia and move to the engineering unit at Prinn, which lay a few miles away in another part of Tripoli. I would stay at Prinn over Christmas and then move up to Homs.

Astounded to hear this, I had no opportunity to question him because suddenly I heard him wishing me luck and telling me he would see me up at Homs in due course.

'Thank you, sir,' I said, and came to attention, saluted and left.

I was completely baffled. What was going on? Why Prinn? Why were they so desperate to get me out of Azizia? Dave Brown would spend Christmas with his friends at Homs; why could I not stay at Azizia till the move after Christmas? I sensed a hidden agenda here, but I could not fathom it out, at least not then.

I scarcely had time to explain things to my Azizia friends before leaving late that afternoon. They seemed as surprised as I and asked what I thought was going on, but I made no comment. At Prinn they gave me a small single room in the mess, and I prepared to stay over Christmas with strangers.

The bombshell of my sudden transfer took its toll and the following morning I awoke with a headache the like of which I had never experienced before, as if a great sledgehammer was banging inside my head and I could scarcely walk because every step was agony. I managed to get hold of some aspirins but they had no noticeable effect. The people at Prinn to be fair did their best to make me welcome, and told me that on that very evening the officers' mess had invited the sergeants' mess to a pre-Christmas party, and that I must be sure to go, dressed in whites.

The last thing I wanted at that moment was to socialise with a lot of people I did not know and whom I would never get to know as I would be leaving Prinn anyway in a few days, but I knew that I could not possibly avoid it. I dressed up and went to the officers' mess, my head absolutely throbbing. As soon as I entered a young subaltern rushed up:

'Hello, there, welcome to the mess, now what can I get you to drink?'

I knew I could not order anything non-alcoholic, though I wanted nothing too strong.

'Er, a rum and Coke,' I said, thinking I could drink a rum drowned in Coca Cola. But with a sinking heart I saw the corporal behind the bar pouring a huge rum and adding a mere dash of Coke!

I took it, and retired to a chair at the side of the dance floor, as the band struck up the military two-step. I took one sip of the drink and with my raging head the room began to swirl around me. I had never been so miserable in all my life and I must have looked really ill.

One or two sympathetic souls passing by asked: 'Are you all right?' No doubt they believed I had had one or two too many to drink.

After a decent interval I slipped away and, head still aching, I fell asleep.

After that I determined to go to Azizia for Christmas Day. I rang them up, got the transport sergeant to fix me some transport and off I went. I had an excellent day with all my friends and stayed at Azizia overnight.

I returned to Prinn next day, where the RSM summoned me and gave me a right rollocking for missing the Prinn Christmas dinner, but I was past caring. My headache had gone, and I should be moving to my new posting with the 6th Royal Tanks the following day, and I had had at least a proper send-off from my friends at Azizia.

I tried to be as philosophical as I could. After all, this was the sort of thing the Army did. I had been looking forward to another long hot summer in Tripoli, with all those good friends, but it was not to be. I would be having instead a long hot summer with the 6th Royal Tanks, 75 miles east along the coast.

7

Teaching the tankies

The Champ, driven by a young trooper from the Royal Tank Regiment, sped away and soon the miseries of Prinn lay behind us. We quickly moved east onto the winding road that would take us from Tripoli to Homs. The road clung to the coast and the blue Mediterranean looked as beautiful as ever on our left and I remembered a little wistfully those delightful summer visits to Piccola Capri. The inland scenery looked brown and rocky enlivened with occasional large prickly pear bushes, but we saw no people. A seventy-five mile journey stretched ahead of us, and it would take a while; we could do no more than 30 to 40 mph on that road. The weather remained fine, despite the fact that it often rained in the winter months, but it seemed cool, almost cold, in the open vehicle though we still wore our full winter BD.

The tankie I noticed wore the jet black beret of the Royal Tank Regiment, and a black lanyard. His belt and gaiters, also black, contrasted sharply with the sandy colour that I had become used to. On each shoulder epaulette I observed the strips of yellow and red ribbon, the familiar flashes of the 6th Royal Tanks. One of my first tasks when I joined my new unit would be to blacken belt and gaiters, and indeed all webbing, and don those red/yellow flashes. The sight of the trooper brought home to me very clearly that I now faced a dramatic change in my military life. The first half of my service overseas had ended and a new era with the 6th Royal Tanks would soon begin.

I had been fond of Tripoli and Azizia. This move had come out of the blue! Why? I thought of the HQ, a bit sloppy and containing men from just about every corps and regiment in the British Army. As an administrative centre it possessed little or no feeling of regimental pride. I remembered those rather untidy morning parades. But I remembered all those close friends as well. Some had been with me since Beaconsfield, and some even since Preston. All that now lay behind me. Ahead stretched life as an education instructor in a proud regiment which I knew would be anything but sloppy. And there would be tanks and other armoured vehicles perhaps. What on earth would it be like?

'Are you national service?' I said by way of conversation to the trooper.

'Yeah.'

'Me too.'

'So how do you find Homs then?'

'Not bad I suppose. Same as most places.'

'Not the same as Tripoli. I've been there since I came out last February. Homs is just a village isn't it?'

Long pause.

'Well it's pretty small. There's not much there. We go down the beach every day. Finish at 1.00, you know. We work quite hard all morning though.'

'Is the beach far?'

'No, just over the road.'

'I'm replacing Sergeant Brown. He's taking my place in Tripoli. We're swopping over.'

'Are you? Why's that then?'

'Well, that's a long story. You know what the Army's like, unpredictable!'

We chatted throughout most of the journey as people do, then after nearly an hour a couple of small buildings came in sight.

'This can't be it,' I thought.

'Halfway house sergeant; we can get a Coke here if you like.'

After our Cokes we pressed on past the same rocky scenery and blue sea, but after nearly another hour we entered the village of Homs. We drove through its centre, and the barracks came into view on the far side. Opposite the entrance I noticed a huge wide sandy bay of great beauty, completely empty of people. We stopped. I gave particulars to the trooper at the entrance. The barrier swung up and in we went.

Beyond the usual large parade square, I could make out some barrack blocks remarkably similar to those at Azizia but perhaps a bit lower, and there seemed to be lots of evergreen trees about the place, but before I could notice more I saw Alain Bain my national service colleague approaching. He spoke with pleasant lowland Scots accent as he guided me towards the mess.

Homs. Entrance to 6RTR Barracks.

'You've timed it well; Mac thought you might be a bit late. You're just in time for lunch. But we'll put your stuff in our room first if you like.'

'Lunch! That's what I need! That journey has given me an appetite. Unlike Prinn I might say. That place was enough to *remove* anybody's appetite.'

'Aye Prinn! What was all that about? Mac told me something about it.'

'I'll tell you later! It'll take a while.'

The sergeants' mess lay over towards the right, with a view in the direction of the square. It was a handsome building in the usual creamy-yellow Italian style, with a garden, secluded because of a wall topped by a neat hedge. It all looked very civilised. We entered a door, and turned left, up a corridor.

'That's the dining-room,' said Alain, pointing to an open door on the left from which emerged the hum of voices. 'Ablutions, right up at the end,' he continued. We paused about halfway down the corridor and he opened a door.

'Here it is. Leave your kit-bag and we'll get a bite to eat. This is my bed,' he said pointing to the bed neatly made up, with a mosquito net in place.

'And that was Dave's bed, now yours,' he continued, pointing to the bed, also made up, on the opposite wall, near the window. 'He's left his mug. That's useful. You'll need one for your morning tea.'

'Morning tea!'

'Oh aye, we get morning tea here. Phil the lance corporal brings it in every morning. They believe in living in style here.'

'Well I'm glad he's left his mug because I haven't seen mine since we came to Libya! It's probably in Azizia somewhere. Dave won't need a mug there. He'll get no morning tea. He won't even have a room in the mess. They'll probably put him in with my old room-mate Alan Goodson. We had a good room, but not in the actual mess. The mess there is nothing like this I can tell you. This, Alain, looks amazingly comfortable.'

I looked approvingly at the spacious well furnished room with its large ceiling fan. A window looked towards the square, with casements opening inwards rather than outwards because of the fine mesh that kept out the flies.

'Aye, it's not so bad. Come on. Lunch.'

I felt at ease in that mess, after Prinn! Prinn had served one useful purpose. It had got the old Azizia life out of my system. So I stood there comparing Homs not with Azizia, but with Prinn. And Homs won by several goals to nil.

Alain introduced me to one and all at the table. Lots of nods followed and one or two asked about Tripoli. Friendliness and informality seemed to be their way with a warm welcome for anyone new to the mess.

We sat at a long, elegant dining table, our meals served to us by a young Arab.

'We've a really good Arab cook. He alternates with an ACC cook. He's good too mind you.' said someone sitting next to me. I felt quite at ease and already part of the community.

Alain and I wandered next into the bar/lounge, accompanied now by Mac (Staff Sergeant J.G. McEwan) who was in charge of the Education Centre at 6RTR Homs. The bar/lounge, with its handsome fireplace, looked ten times bigger than the small bar at Azizia.

'They'll light the fire tonight; they usually do on these winter evenings.'

'I haven't seen a fire since Beaconsfield; it'll be cosy.'

'And this is the good lad who runs this place. Keeps all the Arab helpers on the ball, don't you Phil?'

'Yes sarge,' said Phil, a young, cheerful, lance corporal who seemed to be in charge of the bar.

The lance corporal managed somehow to use the term 'sarge' without giving offence, and it did not seem out of place in the mess at Homs. Informality ruled. Everyone used Christian names and everyone treated the good-natured and popular lance corporal in friendly fashion, often addressing him by his first name too. We called the RSM 'sir' though. And outside the mess we had to take care. Rank then began to count, especially on the square.

We sat down and Mac began to enlighten me about educational provision at Homs. The staff sergeant, yet another Scot, and a regular soldier, came across as totally honest, and totally straight in his dealings.

'I do the maths, and the administration; you two do the rest. That means English, general studies, history, citizenship, you know, all the usual stuff. They're very keen here. The second-in-command, Major Green, supports us completely. He's our boss by the way; he often pops in at the centre; likes to keep abreast, doesn't he, Alain?'

'To see if we've got everything we need,' said Alain.

'Look Mac, I might as well take John round and show him the centre. C'mon, we'll go and get changed, and you can get that webbing seen to. You'll need some shoulder flashes as well. You'll need to be on the ball tomorrow for parade.'

'OK, off you go you two,' said Mac.

We returned to our room, changed into civvies and Alain found a Libyan worker and gave instructions for my belt and gaiters, and indeed all webbing to be blackened.

'It's all done with black boot polish you know, not blanco. They're very good. They make up the beds, and clean the room everyday, and see to dhobying our kit. We usually give them something: they don't get paid much by the Army. Black is the tankies' colour you'll have noticed: everything's black! When you're orderly sergeant you'll need to wear a black sash instead of the red you'll be used to.'

'They didn't wear a sash at all at Azizia!'

My mind went back to Fulwood, and Sergeant Griffiths, and his scarlet sash.

'Well, they're very regimental here. We're in HQ Squadron by the way. And we're on parade every morning except Sundays.'

'Squadron? Is that what we used to call a company?'

'They're called squadrons here, cavalry style. The Tanks form part of the Royal Armoured Corps. Those old cavalry regiments, you know the Dragoons, and the Lancers and all that lot, have tanks these days. They are all part of the RAC now, along with us.'

There was a pause as I tried to take it all in.

'The squadrons parade every day, outside their squadron blocks over there.' He pointed to the square.

'What time?'

'7.30, after breakfast. Reveille's at 6.30.'

'I haven't heard reveille since basic training with the East Lancashire Regiment.'

'Aye, well you'll find it's a bit different here. Like the cavalry, we have a trumpet not a bugle, and they play a different tune! But it'll wake you up all right. You'll hear the trumpeter tonight as well when they lower the flag.'

After we had changed, we wandered off to the education centre. The square teaching room had a handsome blackboard, and lots of desks. Maps hung on the walls.

'That's where it all happens,' remarked Alain.

I had a good look at the files and masses of materials, and booklets, and tried my unpractised hand at the typewriter.

'You can have a good look through all that tomorrow; there'll be plenty of time. And Mac'll go through everything and work out exactly what you'll be doing. You'll carry on Dave's work I expect. Wonder how he's getting on in Tripoli? How is Tripoli, by the way?' I had not been there long, but I had that pleasant feeling that I belonged: a very comforting feeling after being at Prinn for those few days.

I enjoyed an excellent dinner and then a pleasant evening in the mess bar, with a welcome fire flickering in the huge grate. The mess at 6RTR turned out to be a very different place from that at Azizia, with more people in the bar: everyone seemed to be in there. Many I learned were from REME, essential for servicing the tanks, scout cars, half-tracks and so on. They seemed a close knit community, very relaxed with each other, but very welcoming to me. Anyone who arrived and joined the regiment immediately became part of the club and during that first evening everyone said something to me or introduced himself. Some had wives in married quarters; a number had wives back home. A few were single men. Nobby Norman came up and welcomed me to his squadron: he was SSM (squadron sergeant major) of HQ Squadron. He had a son in boarding school back in UK, he explained proudly. As time went on, Nobby would often chat to me about his son's education, and ask me about universities and so on. Meanwhile, Alain kept whispering mysterious things like: 'that's SSM Grist; that's the RQMS; and that's the RSM, Mr Carse. That's SQMS Cranfield, and that's

Sergeant Carney, he's Irish. And that's Sergeant Steer from the Orderly Room. And that's the TQ, he added. 'He believes that sex is a much over-estimated pastime or so he said once in the bar here.'

Completely baffled by all this information, I did manage to stammer out: 'TQ?'

'Technical quartermaster sergeant', replied Alain. 'You'll get to know it all soon enough.'

As they all wore civvies for the evening, it was not easy for me to work out ranks and positions, but soon I would see them all in uniform, most of them with medal ribbons indicating war service in North Africa and Italy, and sometimes France and Germany too. The RSM, quietly spoken and almost scholarly, wore the ribbon of the coveted Burma Star.

The following morning at 6.30 a.m. the trumpet blew reveille to a very different tune from that of the infantry, but one that I would become very used to in the months to come.

Seconds later the door opened, and Phil, the lance corporal came in with a huge pot of tea. He poured some into Alain's mug and said to me 'Tea sarge?'

'Yes thanks corp,' I replied. He half filled the pint mug and I sat up and enjoyed the luxury of the moment.

I had a mad momentary vision of Lance Corporal Cottam, bringing us all cups of tea in that barrack room at Fulwood! He must have been there with a new intake: a good soldier, perhaps a full corporal, but he would not be bringing tea to anyone!

I got dressed, placing the 6RTR red/yellow flashes on my shoulder epaulettes, and donned my belt and gaiters now blackened with boot polish. I now looked, and already felt, part of the regiment.

After breakfast, Alain said: 'We'll march onto to the square, and then you will stand next to me. We have our own little troop of HQ men. Then when it's over we wait for Nobby. He'll dismiss each troop in turn and we'll lead ours off the square. Take care! If we are not good enough he'll bring us round and back to do it again!'

'Right!' I said, hoping I would indeed get it right. It must have been reasonably satisfactory, as he did not ask us to repeat it.

After parade, we made our way to the education centre, and my first day of work with 6RTR. Mac had already arrived; staff sergeants and above did not attend morning parade.

While Alain was next door doing some teaching, Mac went through my duties, and introduced me to the set-up.

'There are one or two doing GCE 'O' Level in maths and English; one's a trooper, but a good lad, and there's someone from the mess; he's pretty good as well. And a corporal. They're all dead keen. Dave took them for English, so you can carry on. There's some of their stuff over there. We've got a scheme we follow. And there are syllabuses you can look through, and plenty of books and worksheets to use. Just see them, chat to them, get to know them, and take it from there. You'll get on fine. Then you can work out with Alain later what you do and what he will do with the general work for the ACE (Army Certificate of Education). We've got some third class and some second class, bigger groups, lots of different groups coming at different times. You can take some, and Alain the others. The third class stuff is pretty basic: English, and current affairs, and general studies about Libya, and so on. Bit about the regiment too. They're all good lads and want to get on and do well. You'll have plenty of time to look over and correct their work while I'm teaching, or Alain's teaching. Anything you want to know, just ask. I'm here to help! OK? It's good to have you here. Now remember John, just ask! OK?'

I had a chat with Alain, and worked out a few things, while Mac took a group for maths. I began to get the hang of it and looked forward to my first session, due to take place the following morning.

'Time for morning coffee. Let's go to the mess, it's 11 o'clock.'

We strolled back to the mess and followed that with a bit more work at the centre.

After lunch I took a stroll round the barracks, to get my bearings and think things over. The three large cream coloured squadron blocks, each with steps leading up to a sort of veranda, reminded me of Azizia. Each squadron block housed a barrack room for its troopers, as well as corporals' rooms, and offices for the squadron commander (a major) and his SSM. I saw a half-track, and an occasional Champ, but in particular I paused to admire the huge Centurion tanks in their compound. Numerous evergreen trees resembled large weeping willows. The administration block, situated near the main entrance, housed the orderly room, the adjutant, and the CO Lieutenant Colonel P.A.L. Vaux, a CO both popular and much respected for his sense of fairness and genuine consideration for the welfare of all under his command.

My life really had changed very dramatically in just a week or so. Two weeks ago I had been happily living at Azizia, sharing a room with Alan Goodson, working in the library with Abdul, Bashir and Don, looking forward to another summer in Tripoli and Piccola Capri, with a large group of friends, and now…

Somehow Homs seemed cut off, a lone unit, near an Arab village and a large deserted beach. Alain Bain was the only other national service sergeant, and the only sergeant in the mess of my age. Unlike Azizia, the barracks served both as home and

Homs. Author in winter uniform.

work place, and people like us, or REME or the cooks, were regarded as being very much part of the regiment As the weeks and months passed I began to realise that this would become a very different experience from that at Tripoli. All ranks bonded as a community: on the beach, on duty, in the mess, at work, wherever. And that community would become important to me too.

* * *

Within a day of arriving at Homs, an immaculately turned out officer complete with black Sam Browne belt had arrived at the centre. Major Green, the regiment's 2i/c, carried his ash plant, a particular stick carried by all tank officers. The ash plant originated in the First World War, when officers used an ash stick to test the firmness of the ground on the Western Front before a tank moved forward. He also wore the ordinary black beret rather than the peaked cap worn by officers from other regiments. Some said that RTR officers wore the black beret because, unlike a cap, it would not get in the way in a small tank, nor would its colour show oil marks.

He welcomed me, asked me if I had settled in, and seemed sure I would do a first-class job. 'I expect you'll be taking over the editorship of The *Homs Weekly Gazette,* our regimental newspaper, taking over where Sergeant Brown left off. It makes a valuable contribution to regimental life: people like to know what's going on.'

Mac indicated that that would be the case.

'Now. Have you got everything you need?'

Mac assured him that we did indeed have all that we needed, and the major left. Having the 2i/c as our particular boss was a privilege for us because he could open all doors and looked after us particularly well. Major Green had a very high reputation within the regiment. In the sergeants' mess they saw him as a very able officer and a potential high flier.

On that second day, I also began to do the instructing that I had been trained for at Beaconsfield. I found it very satisfying: far more so than working at the District Library which had been congenial and interesting in its own way, but not perhaps 'satisfying'.

I first instructed a group of young tankies, mainly national servicemen working for the Army Certificate of Education, Second Class. They came in, stood to attention, sat when told to, and then I held the floor. I had given quite a bit of thought to how I would operate and determined to enjoy it, make a success of it and follow my instincts as well as the training I had received at Beaconsfield. I intended to introduce them to the situation in the Middle East as part of their general studies after having looked at the various materials and plans and strategies. I conducted a question-and-answer session, with the help of a map of the Mediterranean area, partly to see what they knew, and partly to let them participate. Slow to respond at first, by the end of the session they began to relax and take part and, though we did not get very far, I knew that I had gained their confidence and interest. After a week I developed the strategy that I would use in the coming months, built partly on training and instinct but mainly from the experience I built up teaching the soldiers.

Aware that they could be bored out of their minds by a formal lecture I determined not to go in for that: I had suffered myself from a few of those! I knew that the soldiers had to be involved, that they must contribute. If they became involved and interested they would understand and remember. Any idea of expecting them to listen and write and then sit down in the barrack room one night and learn things parrot fashion would have been an absolute disaster: for them because they would make absolutely no progress, and for me because the sessions would become devoid of interest. I also realised, instinctively I think, that these young soldiers must be given confidence: many of them, so good as tank or truck drivers, or wireless operators, or gunners, or swimmers, feared anything that involved writing. They were terrified of looking stupid and of receiving scathing criticism, and I carefully avoided that, and built confidence by giving praise when due and correcting any errors or ignorance very sensitively.

And so I proceeded on those lines, gradually perfecting the technique with practice.

1. I would show them on the map, say, Cyprus, ask them what they thought was going on there, and then just listen. Sometimes there would be a silence, as they waited for me to answer my own question, but I would remain silent, and wait. Sometimes the silence would go on for a full minute, or longer, but I continued to wait.
2. Without exception, someone would eventually say something. I never interrupted him, not even to comment with a 'good' or a 'that's not quite right'. The person talking would finish. Then I would simply thank him without any comments of any sort, and wait again in silence. Eventually, someone else, realising that embarrassing comments would not follow, would add something. And so it would go on.
3. By the end of the session they would have developed, without realising it, the ability just to speak aloud their thoughts knowing the sergeant would never comment in any way. But, they would begin to comment on each other, which of course they did not mind.
4. Eventually, once the group had gelled together, the silences would be very brief: they would begin to contribute. I found it all a matter of confidence.
5. Then, my turn came. I usually referred to all the bits that had been contributed, some of which I had summarised very briefly on the blackboard while the soldier had spoken. I might reject some ideas and build on others and start teaching them, but by that time everybody would have forgotten which trooper had made which point. So if I rejected some points, no particular person felt embarrassed.
6. As the group developed, and as they got to know me and each other, any thought of embarrassment disappeared anyway. And at that stage I might be able to interject and say: 'Well I do not think that is quite right really, what do others think?' At that point we could progress really rapidly. We knew and trusted each other and just wanted to learn.

Some areas of current affairs such as the Suez Crisis needed careful handling. 6RTR had taken part in the Suez business. Some of the regulars, unlike the national servicemen sitting in front of me, had been there. In any case my political opposition to the whole thing was irrelevant, and I never raised it. It would also have been disloyal and subversive. But I found Suez a useful introduction to any explanation of the Arab/Israeli conflict, again without ever revealing my view that the Arabs were in the right and the Israelis in the wrong. They needed to be aware only that these two peoples had a conflict over territory, and that we British had an interest in the matter.

Cyprus, and Suez and problems in Aden, and our presence in Libya interested us particularly. I found them curious also about the divided Germany, the Iron Curtain, and how such situations emerged out of World War II. This became interesting and rewarding to teach and explain, with the full involvement of the class.

As the weeks passed, and I gained more experience I found the job of instructing fascinating and rewarding. I enjoyed contact with all sorts of national servicemen from many parts of the country, though mainly from southern and western counties; they all had differing levels of ability, and widely varying personalities. And, though contemporaries of mine in age, they were very different from me. The Army exempted from education anyone with a clutch of 'O' Levels, so I did not see the sort of people I had known at school. I now met the 80% of the population that my grammar school and university background had cut me off from. They may have been getting an education from the Army, but so was I! At Azizia my contacts outside my own circle had been limited: orderly sergeant and guard commander duties had brought me into contact with others but that was all really. Now, I was actively training ordinary young national service troopers, plus many older regulars who needed our help to gain promotion.

I also taught English. I rapidly discovered that confusion ruled when it came to writing English: confusion, laced with fear. They thought that a malevolent force had invented a mass of incomprehensible rules which defied understanding. Most believed they could never master the complexities of language, with its arbitrary spellings and arcane rules of punctuation.

They summed it up by saying frankly: 'I'm no good at English!'

I decided on three essentials:

1. To remove the fear that English defied understanding.
2. To be very practical in any approach I adopted.
3. To get them involved actively in the process.

I would for example ask a soldier to tell me about the tanks he dealt with on a daily basis, and ask others then to add bits of information on jobs done, and the names of his other workmates. I would ask for a bit of conversation that might be heard in the tank. Then I would with their help write it up on the blackboard, but, with no punctuation in it whatsoever.

I would then ask them what they thought of it.

'Why is punctuation useful? Now I know some of you could punctuate that perfectly with no help from me, but forget that for the moment, and let us put it right together.'

1. First let us underline the speaking bit.
2. Next let us separate it into different statements and put a stroke thus / between each statement.
3. Now, can we improve it by using useful words like 'who' or 'and'?

They began to see punctuation as a useful device to make reading easier. In speech we could use voice inflection or pauses but, when writing we needed some other device. Then the use of full stops and commas and quotation marks could be introduced rather than underlinings or whatever. Somehow this removed their inhibitions about punctuation for it became practical common sense.

In later sessions, once they knew what they were about, we started practical writing, the use of conjunctions, relative pronouns, and useful sentence patterns, without becoming too grammatical or too technical. It seemed to work, and they enjoyed the sessions.

One of them once said to me: 'We don't seem to do much work but we seem to learn an awful lot.' I accepted that as a vote of confidence.

Of course they were well controlled and therefore relaxed students. Army basic training and army discipline had done their work successfully. Now we could enjoy ourselves and make progress. I never had to assert authority or worry about losing authority: those three tapes on my arm were all I needed. No soldier who had been through basic training would ever forget the power that they always represented!

Regular corporals who wanted to gain promotion had to get higher levels of the Army certificates. Some sergeants and even warrant officers wanted 'O' Levels, especially in English, with a view to undertaking high-level correspondence courses (which we could arrange for them) to help with employment when they left the Army. All regulars, including officers, felt a real worry about becoming redundant: some were even made redundant during that time. The British Army faced severe cuts and amalgamation of regiments. The Royal Tanks faced losing three regiments and that meant that 6RTR, when their tour of duty in North Africa came to an end in September, would join 3RTR in Germany. Obviously some officers and senior NCOs must become redundant, and anxiously began to equip themselves for civvy life. I even interviewed at that time a major who wanted a correspondence course to try and fit him for something new. I found the 'O' Level students well-motivated, able, and as keen as young freshmen. They needed plenty of practice with essays, précis, punctuation and sentence analysis. Many found it a worrying time though.

I also taught citizenship, the right to vote and how the legal system worked.

And so, within a few days the pattern was set for my work with the regiment in the months ahead, work which satisfied me greatly. In fact, although I had planned to enter the civil service as a career, I realised that I actually liked teaching more than I had ever thought possible.

I had not been at Homs more than a week when my name went up for orderly sergeant duty, an important duty that would come up quite often. In 6RTR however, as in most units (though Azizia had been an exception) the duty of guard commander was carried out by a full corporal, so I would be spared that particular all-night task.

The orderly sergeant and the orderly officer (a young, often national service, subaltern) mounted guard in the early evening, called out the guard at night and dismounted them the following morning. Throughout those non-working hours they took charge of the barracks, but as the orderly officer usually remained in the officers' mess, outside the barracks, and had to be reached by telephone, the orderly sergeant controlled things in practice. Indeed the sergeant, a senior figure, often with war service, normally guided the youngster through everything and more or less told him what to do.

My case differed. I wore the stripes of a senior NCO but remained a young national serviceman with no more experience than the junior officer. On one occasion however, when the young orderly officer made an error, I suffered a ticking off the following day for allowing it to happen. I should have guided him. After all he was a very junior officer just out from the UK! I, a young conscript and new to the Royal Tanks, but a senior NCO, should take the lead when necessary. This may have been anomalous but we national service sergeants had to live with it.

Being aware of the responsibilities expected of the orderly sergeant especially in a regiment like RTR, I found out all that I could from Alain Bain and the SSM. I also watched carefully the important mounting of the guard, conducted daily with great ceremony right in the middle of the barrack square. It involved members of the guard doing something that up till then I had never even heard of, namely pistol drill! Tank troopers did not carry rifles as did infantrymen: they had pistols in small holsters because rifles within the small confines of a tank would have been a nuisance. I, however, trained in the infantry knew rifle drill but nothing at all about 6RTR's pistol drill. However, as Alain pointed out, I did not actually have to do the drill, merely give three orders: to draw the pistol, present it, and return it to the holster.

So, having carefully memorised the three orders I donned the impressive black sash of the orderly sergeant, grabbed the long stick of office that he always carried, and prepared for the guard mounting. At that moment, I had a brief vision of Sergeant Griffiths who, on the square at Fulwood, had always worn his red sash and swung his stick of office with great aplomb and thought to myself : 'If he could see me now, mounting guard out here in distant foreign parts.'

It all went well and without errors. I marched them onto the middle of the square. I observed the young orderly officer at the far side. As he began to march smartly onto the square, I set off marching towards him. We halted facing each other, and I saluted. He returned the salute.

'Guard ready for your inspection, sir!'

I made a smart about turn, and we marched together, side by side towards the guard standing to attention.

'Gua-ard. Open order march!' I shouted.

On my next order I was relieved to see them draw their pistols with perfection. We inspected them. They were of course immaculate because I had previously inspected them before coming onto the square, but this did not prevent the officer going through the necessary motions, as they always did, pulling slightly at something here, and brushing off an imaginary fleck of dust there.

Then I gave the order to replace the pistols into their holsters.

'Gua-ard. Close order march!'

'Right turn!'

And off we went to the guardroom.

I had survived the first of many 6RTR guard mounting ceremonies, watched usually by the critical eyes of the occasional officer or SSM or even the RSM. And, as I received no comments later, I assumed that the guard and I had passed muster. It had all been very different from the little affair we had conducted outside the guardroom at Azizia. As orderly sergeant I had to patrol the Homs camp from time to time, and look in at the guardroom. Later I had to close the NAAFI, and the corporals' mess bar, and then, with a tremendous sense of power, the sergeants' mess bar, though one had to ask the RSM or senior warrant officer present: 'Permission to close the bar, sir?'

Being young, and new to the regiment, I still found it incredible what power that black sash and long stick seemed to give me over the barracks. It seemed as if the whole of the 6RTR were within my power for those few hours

* * *

During the summer of 1958, I had experienced my first trip into the desert. That journey to Ghadames had been fabulous. In early 1959 I experienced my second excursion.

Our troops had remained in Libya to offer some protection to King Idris who feared Nasser's Egypt and Arab nationalism, but as a by-product we, in turn, gained a valuable and unique training ground for our soldiers, and particularly for tanks. And so, in February , we heard that the whole regiment would leave Homs for about six weeks exercise in the desert. We too from the education centre, would join them and carry on with our normal duties. Only a small base unit would be left at Homs. An advance party first moved off to set up camp. Then, after a few days, all the Centurion tanks, half tracks, and scout cars, Champs, Land Rovers, water carriers, and three-tonners followed, including Alain and me. We pressed ever on farther and farther into the desert and eventually sighted camp on flat, sandy, stony ground. It felt almost like being at sea. The desert stretched to every horizon. We alighted from our vehicle and looked around to find rows and rows of bell tents, neatly arranged in squadrons. Other larger tents housed administration areas, the sergeants' mess and other messes. I also noticed in between the rows of tents several pipes sticking out of the ground, each about three feet long, curved at the top a little bit like air funnels on board ship. I could not imagine their function till I observed a trooper using one later in the day: they were urinals, army desert-style. Eventually we found the education centre: a large square tent, its sides lifted up for coolness, containing all the furniture we had arranged to be sent out: desks, tables, cupboards, all our filing systems, typewriter and materials of every sort. We had spent several days supervising the loading up of just about our whole set-up, and now began sorting it out for work in a day or so. We could not cease instructing merely because the regiment was on exercise. Those detailed to come to us at various times would not be excused and our work would continue. Alain and I set off to find HQ Squadron and our bell tent, and found SSM Norman getting things organised with his customary efficiency. 'You're over here,' he called out so we walked towards one of the tents. Pleasantly gloomy inside, I was amazed to see that it had been furnished with two army beds, complete with mattresses, sheets, pillows, and mosquito nets. I had expected to have some sort of rough palliasse on the ground at best! We each had a small bedside locker.

'Very nice!' I said.

'Any fool can be uncomfortable!' he replied, speaking with all the experience of one who had served in the Eighth Army in that very desert during the war. He glanced meaningfully towards the area where the young subalterns were billeted.

Later we enjoyed a very nice lunch in the mess tent and a cool drink in the bar tent. In our own tent, before turning in, we took a glass from our bottle of Haig's Dimple, a rather special whisky, a gift from Mac. It crossed my mind that this 6RTR exercise would be a lot more comfortable than our excursion the previous year when we had slept out of doors in a sandstorm.

I confirmed this next morning after being awakened by reveille; I saw a hand pulling aside the flap of our tent, and in came Phil, our lance corporal, with our morning tea!

That day saw us sorting things out in the education tent for we had to be ready for our instruction duties.

'Look out!' said Alain. 'Here comes the 2i/c.'

Major Green, as immaculate as ever, strode towards us. We came to attention and saluted as he entered the tent.

'At ease! I just wanted to make sure that you have everything you need,' he said.

'Yes, sir, everything's in order, sir,' said Mac in his pleasant Scots accent.

'Good, good. I've arranged for all normal education classes to go on as usual, so there should be no problems.' Off he went.

'What in God's name did he want?' said Mac in the gruff ungracious way he sometimes adopted when talking about commissioned officers.

During the days that followed, quiet reigned when most people left on exercise with the tanks, but we continued our work every morning. What an experience to stand in that tent and instruct our pupils in all the various skills that we had to impart, even if at times they seemed a bit listless in the increasing heat!

Then in the evening we heard in the bar all about the exploits of the tanks on the training ground.

Everything (guard duties, orderly sergeant duties and so on) continued as normal, even in that unusual desert setting. But, as always in the Army, we adapted to it and soon found it normal to be out there in the middle of nowhere, instructing soldiers in such mysteries as the EOKA in Cyprus.

Fascinating as I found our work out there in the desert, it is always interesting to have a diversion from the norm, and one soon came my way. Every so often some troopers were allowed a break, and three large trucks would set off for Homs under the command of a sergeant so that the men could have baths and a bit of relaxation before returning later on the same day. The journey took at least an hour. After a couple of weeks, my turn came, and I supervised the loading up of each three-tonner with troopers. I climbed into the leading truck and told the driver to get going. We bumped along rough terrain flanked by odd bits of vegetation from time to time. After about thirty minutes things seemed to warm up. Eventually it became unbelievably hotter than it should have been, and when I touched the casing of the engine which protruded into the cab I almost burned my finger.

'That's badly over-heating. It'll be a miracle if it doesn't seize up!' I said.

'It's hotter than it should be,' agreed the driver.

'Make sure you get it checked out before we return tonight.'

'Yes s'arnt,' he said. 'I'll see to it.'

'See that you do,' I said.

Everyone got out at the barracks and I ordered them to report for the return journey at 7.30 pm. The camp seemed strangely empty and still but I managed to get a bath and a cool drink in the mess. At 7.30 the troopers arrived, fairly drunk and merry and clambered aboard. Off we set. The truck seemed to be in good order and as it gradually grew darker we trundled along into the desert.

I could see the following trucks in the wing mirror, but after 30 minutes or so I noticed something wrong. I thought I heard something, and the third truck appeared to be stationary and indeed it gradually disappeared from sight.

'Stop!' I ordered. 'There's something the matter with the third truck!'

I got out and went back to the second truck.

'He's broken down s'arnt.'

'Back up!' I said.

Both trucks backed up, not easy on that terrible road in the dark. And at the same time I realised that the broken down truck had been the leading truck on the way out: the one with the over-heating engine.

'That truck's the one you and I came out in: did you get that engine checked out as I told you?'

'Well, I thought it would be all right after it had cooled, so ...'

I showed my anger, confronted with a broken-down truck full of drunken young troopers, in the middle of nowhere, in the dark. I swore at him, shouted at him, threatened to put him on a charge the moment we got back to camp for disobeying an order.

When we reached the stricken truck, I found its driver examining the over-heated engine. It had seized up, and he could get no life out of it: it needed serious attention. We could not possibly carry the troopers from the third truck in the other two trucks, each being already full to capacity. In any case I could hardly leave a truck abandoned in the desert.

I allowed the troopers to get out of the trucks to stretch their legs, hoping none would go missing.

'We'll have to tow it!' I said. 'Get the tow-rope!'

I half expected him to say: 'What tow-rope?' In fact however he came back with one.

They fixed up the tow-rope, I managed to shepherd the merry and fairly drunken young troopers on to the trucks again and we set off at about half speed, eventually reaching the camp, very late. My driver fell silently contrite. I further berated him but as we arrived safe and sound, I relented and told him that as all had ended well after all, I would not be putting him on a charge, but told him to report the fault and ensure repairs.

I mentioned it to the SSM suggesting that 6RTR trucks should be kept in better order, with which he agreed. I told him that I had decided not to charge the driver but that it would do him no harm to have the benefit of a few more choice words from the sergeant major, something I knew Nobby would enjoy dishing out the following morning.

6RTR stayed in the desert for six weeks and towards the end it began to feel like a permanent posting. Like everyone else I began to look forward to going 'home' to Homs, and getting down to the beach, but we heard that we were not going to escape without holding a huge mounted parade and that no less a person than Major General H.R.B. Foote, holder of the Victoria Cross and Colonel Commandant of the Royal Tank Regiment, would take the salute. He had planned a particular visit to see 6RTR because this would be 6RTR's last desert parade. British overseas commitments had diminished and the government had already planned large cuts in military expenditure. The regiment would be returning home in the autumn, prior to moving to Germany and amalgamation with 3RTR. The future now demanded a small highly professional army and the end of national service.

We provided the general with a caravan, borrowed from Tripoli, and a batman, Lance Corporal Ducker, a real old soldier who had once actually served in the RN in a submarine! While the general and the tanks were out on exercise, the old lance corporal, a Maltese, showed great enterprise making a few 'ackers' showing the general's medals, including the VC, to all soldiers prepared to pay a small fee! I later learned that our colonel actually knew all about it and saw the funny side of it all, but Ducker never knew that the colonel knew!

Unsure exactly what a mounted parade involved, I learned that I would be commanding a water-carrier and would take the salute as we drove past the general. 'You stand with your head out of the roof opening and take the salute, eyes right, as you drive past!' stated the SSM, when I made some inquiries. One of the charming things about 6RTR was that everyone became an integral part of the regiment and took part in everything. They assumed that we knew all about the ways of the Royal Armoured Corps and the Tanks. I had often wondered why army trucks always seemed to have a circular opening above the passenger seat; now I knew.

General Foote addresses 6RTR in the desert.

Desert parade.

The CO and the tanks would lead the way, with the tank commanders standing up to take the salute, and every possible vehicle, from scout cars to my humble water-truck would take part in the parade. They stressed what a great occasion lay ahead.

Before the parade, the general inspected us. We took our position a few rows back, on slightly raised ground with an excellent view of rows of subalterns, standing to attention with their ash plants at their sides. As the general passed quickly along the front row, we clearly saw a young officer running to the second row and giving, or returning, an ash plant to a brother officer before the general reached that point: clearly they were one ash plant short! My mind raced back to Beaconsfield and the boy with the missing kit! No wonder we could never fool anybody! Everybody, including I daresay the general himself, had been through it all and knew all about missing kit.

Eventually it was time for the great drive past. My driver being an experienced Irish regular trooper, I felt in good hands.

'Been on one of these mounted parades before?' I asked. To which he just grunted, albeit with an Irish accent.

As soon as the tanks moved off to an impressive roar blanking out all sound, an enormous cloud of dust and sand arose; every vehicle including us slowly followed in the designated order and you could see absolutely nothing. How the driver found his way I shall never know. I had my head out of the top and had a wonderful view of the dust. In the murky gloom I could just make out the commander of the vehicle in front turning eyes right and saluting what could vaguely be made out to be a platform where the general stood. So with eyes right I saluted till we passed.

The terrific occasion gained extra resonance from all the dust and sand, and when I think of all the distinguished war veterans who took part, not least the VC-holding general taking the salute, I felt rather proud to participate. The general thanked everyone for the parade, calling it 'excellent – what I could see of it!'

Shortly after that, the enormous task of packing up and returning to Homs took place, and gradually we returned back to normal. Alan and I celebrated with a trip into Homs for a dish of Zacchi's superb spaghetti bolognese.

8

Keeping the flag flying

Warm weather returned by the end of March and soon after returning to Homs we were in our KD shorts and tops once again. We began to make daily afternoon visits to the beach and my thoughts strayed back nostalgically to Tripoli and those delightful cycle rides to Piccola Capri. I would have given a lot just then for another Tripoli summer in the company of all those good friends from Azizia. The Homs summer had yet to cast its spell over me, though in time I would find its charms no less seductive than those of Tripoli.

At Homs the beach lay close at hand, just across the road from our main gate and down some steps. To the left was the village, with its harbour wall. The beach itself extended for a mile or so till it reached the ruined Roman city of Leptis Magna at the far end. It was a superb beach of soft white sand facing a vividly blue sea and framed on the landward side by tall palms. No other buildings of any kind existed apart from the barracks itself, and the village, and a small kiosk/hut selling cold drinks.

The people on the beach seemed to be in the main young national service soldiers. Older regulars and their wives did not come down very often, and their older children of course attended the Army secondary school in Tripoli. We clustered together in the spot considered safe for bathing. The regiment had anchored a raft in deep water a little way out and we loved to swim to it, sunbathe a bit or swim around it, and then swim back. Otherwise people splashed around and generally enjoyed themselves. The rest of the huge beach remained totally empty. Once we tried bathing a little way down towards Leptis but currents proved very dangerous indeed. I recall standing up to my waist in water only a few yards out to sea and finding it almost impossible to walk back. I had to launch myself towards the shore half swimming and half walking: the pull of the current terrified me. So with good reason we all kept together in the area around the raft. Indeed I heard a possibly apocryphal tale of an Arab drowned while bathing during the summer of the previous year, and another told of a very strong swimmer who swam out to sea and could not get back because of the current. He had to swim several miles down the coast before reaching land.

Alain and I would sometimes take with us his portable chess set and enjoy a game followed by a dip in the sea and maybe a snooze in the sun but more often we socialised with the corporals and troopers. Other young national sergeants did not exist at Homs and rank did not count for much on the beach. Most of us of course were national servicemen and there was something rather special about that national service army. We came from every possible background, and lived close together for a couple of years whether we liked it or not. Our conscript army, unlike our much vaunted comprehensive schools, was truly comprehensive. Public schoolboys really did rub shoulders with lads from the slums. Northerners did get to know southerners. Liverpudlians did learn to love Geordies. Scots did realise that the Welsh existed, and the Welsh learned that many besides the Welsh could sing. Of course today's highly professional British army is second to none and understandably glad not to be made up of mere conscripts, but it has nevertheless lost something valuable. We were a people's army, a citizens' army: something not to be despised. One young lad on that beach, educated at Eton, mingled happily with clerks from the orderly room, tank drivers, wireless operators including another public schoolboy, a Scot from Strathallan School, gunloaders, cooks, mechanics, all doing their 'two years' as we used to say in those far off days. We enjoyed the company of young regulars too, including two rough diamonds whose photograph I still possess: Corporal Patey from London I think, and Lance Corporal 'Dinger' Bell from Newcastle. All of us, national servicemen and regulars, in spite of our varied backgrounds, seemed bound together by that family regimental feeling so strong within 6RTR.

Often we just lay there and talked. We talked about everything, about the Army and national service, and about what we planned to do after we got out, and so on. We all compared notes of course about the horrors of basic training. I regaled them with tales about the high life in Tripoli, a town mostly unknown to the troopers of 6RTR, until they forced me to admit that my stories of the high life were much exaggerated. Everyone on that beach seemed relaxed about the Army and its ways and we laughed a lot. Like me, they had adapted to service life. They would not actually have said so, but they had clearly enjoyed themselves in 6RTR. We talked of going home because that time lay ahead for all of us. 6RTR would sail home in September. My service too would end in September, and Alain's in August. On the beach in Tripoli that previous summer, time had stretched out before me; now, at Homs, we all saw the end approaching and our mood became reflective as we pondered the future.

No newcomers arrived on the beach that summer, except a new chaplain, a good mixer who joined us regularly. He looked unhealthily white at first compared with the rest of us because we were all dark brown still from the previous summer, but he soon acquired his tan.

At about 4 o'clock, Alain and I would wander up to the mess for that glorious army feast of hot tea and sandwiches, and then a shower and perhaps a brief lie down before getting changed into more formal attire for dinner.

Sometimes after dinner, in the cool of the evening, we would stroll along the beach towards Leptis. Alain took the opportunity on such occasions to introduce me to the mysteries of rugby. He came from Galashiels where rugby is *de rigueur* for everyone. I came from an area of the north where it was largely unheard of, except as an esoteric activity played at certain public schools. I learned about passing the ball back, and he would even bring along his rugby ball and we would run down the beach passing to each other.

'Speed is everything!' said he.

'Speed? I can outrun you any time,' said I somewhat optimistically.

'Come on then!'

When he easily outstripped me I began to see why he played for the regiment. It was not beneath him however to use his considerable talents as a teacher to introduce me to the tactics and purposes of the game, something which I must say I felt glad of in later life when I lived in South Wales, and made my way up to Murrayfield with a load of Welsh colleagues to watch Scotland beat the Welsh in the 1960s.

Occasionally we wandered off into the village, glanced at the few little Italian shops and perhaps called in at the NAAFI shop. Homs could not compete with Tripoli but it had its own particular charm. We certainly enjoyed a cup of tea and a piece of cake at the Church of Scotland canteen. Some delightful Scottish ladies ran the place and everyone liked to drop in for something to eat, and a bit of cheerful, albeit mature, female company; it became a little touch of the UK (or at least of Scotland) and somewhere non-military and non-Libyan, where all ranks could meet and socialise on equal terms. Everyone regarded it as an important centre in our rather 'cut-off' Homs life. The colonel, always mindful of looking after the welfare of his young national service troopers, had encouraged the church canteen ladies to hold a fortnightly dance. He and his wife encouraged married officers and sergeants to attend with their wives, otherwise there would have been no women there! The troopers could and did do a bit of dancing but those who abstained still enjoyed the evening out. These 'club-nights'

Homs. Panorama.

proved popular and successful events, albeit, in the spirit of the Church of Scotland, alcohol-free!

Our favourite calling-in place was Zacchi's, where we would treat ourselves to a meal and a bottle of wine. On entering the popular café, Zacchi, a very jolly black Libyan or Sudanese, with curly black hair, always gave a huge smile of welcome. He loved to chat and he made absolutely delicious spaghetti bolognese.

We also occasionally enjoyed, perhaps a bit daringly for those days, an after-dark naked dip off the pier, to cool off on those very warm evenings.

Most evenings however, we spent in the mess. They always called Alain Bain 'Jock' and me too for some reason: I think they just assumed that all education personnel were Scottish! Sometimes however they called us 'schoolie', especially 'Brummie', the cheerful sergeant from the stores who I always thought must be at least sixty years of age, but who, despite his row of medal ribbons, surely could not have been! The tankie and REME sergeants on the whole were an erudite lot, able men and mechanically minded but they also liked discussing military strategy, politics and so on. On such occasions Sergeant 'Prof' Jones often held the floor earnestly explaining something to those prepared to listen. They also knew also how to relax, enjoy themselves and just have fun amongst friends.

Sometimes we, the sergeants and warrant officers, held a dance. The regiment had a nice little band, 'The Rhythm Rascals', in which the new chaplain showed great skill at playing the accordion. Wives attended of course and dancing went on but many of us merely drank and talked to the music. People would tell me exaggerated tales of the exploits of David Brown and how sometimes he drank neat gin. I preferred mine with ice and tonic or better still in my favourite drink from Azizia and Piccola Capri, the John Collins.

Occasionally we received distinguished visitors including Christopher Soames the War Minister, on a visit to 6RTR, called in for a chat and drink in the mess.

On one occasion the officers invited us to very grand social evening at their mess in the fine Italian villa up the road towards Leptis Magna. We all dressed up in number 3 dress or mess dress, and the officers looked magnificent with their dark blue cummerbunds and white jackets. Flunkies held aloft silver dishes filled with superb food. We lived well in the sergeants' mess but the life-style of the officers was like something from the pre-war days of empire. And why not? I shall always remember that feast.

And so I settled down to the good life, Homs style, in my second summer abroad.

* * *

Early on, when I had only been in Homs a few days, Alain had mentioned the great Roman city of Leptis Magna. 'It is one of the finest remaining Roman cities in the whole of the Mediterranean area: perhaps the best anywhere. We'll walk along the beach and have a look at it if you like.'

It sounded like a good idea, and an exciting one. I had read Modern History and Politics at university. Modern history meant all history since the fall of the Roman Empire but that had not prevented the university insisting that we all study Roman Britain. This may have been because we had on the staff one of the country's most distinguished historians of Romano-British history: Professor Ian Richmond. So distinguished was he that his alma mater Oxford University eventually created a special chair for him, in order to tempt him back. I could well recall how he took us around the Roman Wall in Northumberland, or Hadrian's Wall as everyone seems to call it nowadays, and brought it to life talking for ten minutes or more on even the tiniest scratch! Leptis Magna, thought I some four years later, must be at least as good as Hadrian's Wall.

It was better!

Leptis had been founded by Phoenician colonists from Sidon in modern Lebanon, later joined by people from Tyre who traded with the African interior. The city had sided with the senators of Rome against Julius Caesar, so when Caesar triumphed he taxed the city 300,000 measures of oil annually, a heavy tribute.

However, as a free city governed by its own magistrates, it rose to *colonia* status under Trajan. Later, Emperor Septimius Severus

(193-211 AD), born in York, favoured the city, and most of the fine buildings date from his time. However, towards the end of the Roman Empire Leptis declined because of incursions of desert peoples such as the Garamantes, the Austuriani and the Levathae, and the great harbour silted up. The Byzantine Emperor Justinian tried to revive its fortunes in the 6th century, and built churches there as well as at Sabratha, but with the surge of Islam from the east after the 7th century Leptis died.

The port and easily identifiable quays lie on the east bank of the Cinyps (now called Wadi Lebda) and it was easy to envisage Roman ships embarking from there with gold, perfumery, ivory and with wild beasts intended for the Roman games.

The urban area, called Neapolis (New City) lay on the west bank of what had become Wadi Lebda. My first impression, as we entered the urban area was of a forest of stone pillars, largely in ruins, but reaching to the sky everywhere it seemed, and then arches, and statues, and wonderful roads lined with more pillars. As the only ones there, we explored at will. Over the course of many visits, we often wandered along just for the walk, and then made our way up into the city. We just could not resist it. The vividly blue Mediterranean formed the backdrop, and there we stood in Leptis, testimony to the greatness that was Rome. And there was so much of it. One could feel the presence of those Roman soldiers who used to walk those streets as we walked them nearly 2000 years later.

The well-preserved theatre impressed me enormously, with its tiers of stone steps rising up from a semi-circular stage. Here on these stone steps the Roman citizens had sat so long ago watching the actors perform. The view from those tiers of 'seats' was superb with ruined pillars of other buildings stretching out behind the stage towards the blue sea. I thought of the fall of Rome, and the so-called Dark Ages that followed, and the simple desert people who now inhabited the land.

'All this,' I remarked, 'and how often do we see anyone? Hardly anybody ever seems to visit it.'

'Aye, well,' said Alain. *'Full many a gem of purest ray serene the dark unfathom'd caves of ocean bear.'*

I joined in: *'Full many a flower is born to blush unseen, and waste its sweetness on the desert air.'*

Leptis Magna. Apollo.

We had the benefit of a small book in the education centre which described the various parts of the city, and we used to take it along on our numerous visits and try to identify the sites. Tall columns surrounded the magnificent sports ground leading straight into the magnificent baths. The pool and cold, warm, and hot rooms could be clearly identified by anyone with a slight knowledge of Roman civilisation. An impressive colonnaded street led from the forum and basilica, other outstanding features.

Two things stand out in my memory: rows and rows of latrines, clearly identifiable keyhole shapes cut into the stone; and also the stall where the butcher cut his joints, chops and steaks, with clearly marked grooves in the smooth stone where the chopper had fallen on the meat. We examined arches, great walls, and the harbour. The sheer size and scale of the ruined city struck us with wonder. How lucky I felt to be based so close to such a tremendous piece of history.

Early in the summer I was summoned to see the colonel himself, a man of great courtesy, even to a young national serviceman of no consequence such as I. He asked how I was and what I hoped to be doing on returning to civilian life. He then went on to say that some military VIPs would arrive soon. They were in Cyprus, heading for Tripoli. They had particularly asked to come up to Homs in order to visit Leptis Magna. He reminded me that I was a historian and asked how I felt about guiding the visitors around the site. Frank Hugo, Head of the Army Junior School at Homs, usually acted as guide but could not always be available.

'Sergeant Bain and I have visited the site a few times. I am no expert but I would be glad to show them round.'

And so I became an occasional army guide to the ruins. Two men and two women duly came. For the first time, I actually rode to the city by road in army transport. My guests asked constant questions about Rome, and the Romans in North Africa, and Tripoli and Sabratha. They seemed to think I was some sort of expert and constantly asked if I had been to this place in Egypt, or that place in Palestine, but I had to disappoint them on those.

I enjoyed it, and drew upon my wider knowledge of Rome and its civilisation to put the city in some sort of context. Looking back I think I may have exhausted them though. I was young and used to the great heat of the summer; they were middle-aged and had a look of exhaustion at times, and when I suggested that they might like five minutes rest they always jumped at the chance. Well perhaps I should say 'sat down' at the chance.

After that, on a number of occasions throughout the summer, I guided distinguished visitors around the site, and when I eventually received my certificate of national service with its testimonial, it referred to Sergeant Kelly making use of his 'historical knowledge in showing visitors around the Roman ruins at Leptis Magna'.

On the strength of that, perhaps I can return one day, and get myself a retirement job as an 'English Guide' to Leptis.

* * *

Shortly after returning from our desert exercise Mac had complained of feeling unwell, and he certainly looked poorly under his tan. Eventually they diagnosed him as suffering from jaundice, and swept him off to BMH (British Military Hospital) in Tripoli. Alain and I now took charge of the education centre.

As Alain was senior to me, having been called up a month earlier and having been with the 6RTR for longer, we agreed that he should miss the morning parade, head straight for the centre and start on the mail as Mac had done. It seemed sensible: sensible to us at any rate.

The following morning I paraded with my little troop but without Alain.

'Sergeant Kelly, where is Sergeant Bain?' roared Nobby Norman, HQ SSM, whose eagle eye always spotted any absence, and whose voice had a clear note of menace in its tone.

'Opening up the education centre, sir! Staff Sergeant McEwan is away sick!'

'Go and fetch him!'

'Yes, sir' I said, and marched off.

I found Alain opening the mail.

'Nobby's in a right state. You are required on parade! I've been sent to fetch you. Come on quickly!'

We marched on together.

Nobby sounded ratty that morning. He berated the troopers about the state of the squadron blocks and the filthy windows.

'Don't tell me you need something to clean the windows with! Use newspaper, the best window cleaning material in existence. And you've got enough comics in there to clean every window in Homs!'

Then, as our little troop marched off, he screamed out, 'Right wheel,' and brought us back for not being smart enough.

Round we went again, and back we came again till at last we satisfied him. It was all part of the fun of the morning parade, and something he did from time to time. We knew that in the mess that evening he would be a different man, chatting about his son, and treating us almost like sons. And we would call him 'Nobby' rather than 'sir'.

Sometime earlier Alain had badly injured his arm playing rugby, leaving me as the one able-bodied person in the education centre. Our department had to cope with quite a bit of administration. We sent off letters just about every day. We received countless memos from the SO2 in Tripoli, materials from 68AEC, instructions from the examination people and so on. I rapidly taught myself to type efficiently and took charge of most of that. We had to answer the phone, keep in touch with the orderly room, and do all the things Mac had done. It made the job more interesting, as we could now see it all in the round and in context, and the experience taught me something about efficient administration.

We had to learn quickly because the annual admin. inspection was imminent: a detailed inspection of the whole regiment by Brigadier Laing himself from HQ in Azizia. We began to receive a stream of visitors making us very nervous. First came the adjutant, Captain Weaving. He wanted to check our files and systems, and shouted out as he left: 'Get this whole place painted!' Then, a day or so later, without warning, the SO2, Major Downes, strode into the centre, catching me unawares and on my own. I had not seen him since that interview just before

Christmas and I felt momentarily nonplussed but he expressed his pleasure with reports on my work. He wanted to make sure that we had the inspection in our sights. He looked around and issued a few orders for us to carry out. He also wanted me in Tripoli for a big meeting at 68 AEC as a colonel was coming over from HQ in Cyprus to address us all. 'Sergeant Bain had better stay here to look after the centre.'

Meanwhile we continued to teach all our groups, and tried to fill in for Mac's groups. Life had become unusually busy.

The following week, I set off eagerly for my trip to Tripoli, a driver and a Land Rover having been made available at my request. I relished the opportunity to escape from our now hectic education centre and, anyway, Dave Brown had rung up to say he had some ideas for a joint holiday which we could discuss when I came down to the meeting.

Despite leaving early, we arrived late as we always found it difficult to gauge the time, and Homs lay a good 75 miles to the east of Tripoli. I told the driver to amuse himself and try to get some refreshment, and hurried to the lecture room for my first visit to 68 AEC since we planned that desert trip in the previous year.

'Ah, Sergeant Kelly from Homs,' said the lieutenant colonel from Cyprus, 'Come in, come in. Good journey down?'

I spotted Major Jefferies, and WO1 Luffman, and those particular friends, Dave Brown and Lawrence Laidlaw who had been with me since Fulwood days in Preston. Dave now worked at 68 AEC and Lawrence had taken over my old job at the Library. I wondered how he liked working with Don. I spotted Clive Canton, the Welsh boy, and others who like Clive had been with me at Beaconsfield though not Preston. John Curtiss who had been in such trouble over lost kit in Beaconsfield, looked pensive as he often did, and my mind momentarily went back to that disastrous incident we had shared with the inflatable raft at Piccola Capri. Next to him sat the cheerful young lad from Wolverhampton, Bob Harrison, who had come in at 18 and had a place waiting for him at Cambridge. In a year or so, aged 20, he would be amongst the dreaming spires. We had all thought him very young and naïve but when he reached university and mixed with new 18-year-olds just out of school, they would see him as a well-travelled ex-soldier. I noticed too John Percival, the bacteriologist from Rowlands Gill.

I pondered over what it might be like teaching at 68AEC; it now seemed a big place compared with our set-up at Homs. And did they all still go to the beach on bicycles? I hardly heard the colonel as I sat musing about the past. I thought of all those non-education people with whom I had become so friendly at Azizia and on the beach, people like Alan Goodson and John Heppenstall. How I missed them all. Meanwhile the colonel continued with his address, stressing the importance of our work and so on.

During morning coffee, I managed to have a chat with everyone there, including Dave Brown whom I had replaced at 6RTR. For me the lecture had turned out to be a welcome break from the pressures at Homs.

'John! How are things up there? How are you getting on with Nobby? How's Alain Bain? Still fanatical about rugby? I quite miss it all, but I'd rather be here.'

'He's damaged his arm, and of course Mac is in BMH in Tripoli. So we've taken complete charge. And I'm the only fully fit one there! And we have the big admin. inspection coming up soon. It's a right mess! At this moment, I am glad to be here as well.'

'Never mind all that. Listen, I've had an idea. You know I mentioned leave. We've all got plenty to come. We could go up to Misurata for a week, and stay in a hotel. It would be really interesting I think, and a complete break. What d'you think?'

'Misurata? Isn't that beyond Homs, further east?'

'Yes, I remember some people talking about it in the Royal Tanks. A bus goes up there along the coast from Homs. There's a nice little Italian hotel there.'

'Sounds good, yes, let's go. But not till our admin. inspection is over. I'll be ready for a holiday after that!'

'OK, I'll give you a ring at your centre. Meanwhile, you inquire about leave. There shouldn't be a problem. I'll come up to Homs and stay the night in the mess, renew a few old acquaintances, and we could leave the next day.'

And so a little holiday was fixed.

I chatted too with Lawrence Laidlaw. I mentioned my responsibilities with the *Homs Weekly Gazette* but Lawrence trumped me with news of his new job as sub-editor of the *Tripdist Gazette,* a substantial newspaper within Tripolitania District. He saw to distribution, and helped with layout and advertising, visiting shops and bazaars all over Tripoli to discuss terms over bitter black coffee. Apart from that Lawrence had been assisting a Maltese boy with his English and Brigadier Laing's son, Anthony, with his maths!

At the end of the morning I prepared to go back.

'Keep the flag flying,' shouted the colonel as I left to seek out my driver and our Land Rover.

Then came the day of the big 6RTR inspection. Alain and I waited patiently for our turn. As they approached we stood to attention side by side. I could see the Brigadier, a short man, but confident, authoritative, and a bit intimidating. He approached with a huge entourage of officers, including our colonel and the 2/ic. We were introduced. The Brigadier spoke briefly to me, and then, spotting Alan and his broken arm, proceeded to have a long conversation about rugby and Alain's brilliance as the Regimental Fifteen's stand-off which the Brigadier greatly admired and enjoyed. This took up all the time they could afford to spend with us, and with the briefest of glances inside our centre they swept on.

I said to Alain: 'Thank God for your rugger and injured arm. We've passed.'

* * *

Dave came up to Homs as planned and stayed overnight. We packed a few casual things, shorts, summer shirts and so on, made sure we had a bit of money, and made our way into Homs and waited for the bus. It was well into the 90s, but such temperatures held no terrors for us by then.

A small group of Arabs also waited for the single-decker bus, looking rather curiously at us as we stood there. We paid the driver and clambered aboard. Libyans wearing long shirts and loose trousers and sometimes long robes, occupied about half of the seats in the swelteringly hot bus. They all chatted continually in Arabic.

'It's going to be a hot journey,' I said thinking that it must be at least 120 degrees in that bus.

'Och, it's not so bad, and we'll be there in an hour.'

The road followed the coast to begin with and soon after setting off we stopped to pick up a crowd of people and animals waiting at the side of the road. An enormous argument broke out between the driver and the would-be passengers about the fare, or perhaps he was not keen on the animals: we could not tell. Then he allowed a few on. After more shouting and gesticulating a few more got on. After about ten minutes we set off again at a stately 25 miles per hour.

'It'll be more like two hours at this rate,' I murmured.

And then we stopped again, and again a huge argument arose, before, eventually, more passengers got on.

Several stops later the bus began to heave with people Somehow or other however, it always managed to absorb the load, and as we drove on into less inhabited areas we picked up fewer and fewer people. Although the journey did take longer than the estimated hour, I found it totally fascinating to glimpse aspects of Libyan life that had eluded us so far.

We saw the sea from time to time but generally we passed through rocky, sandy scenery, with occasional trees and orchards, and then eventually we began to pull into the attractive town of Misurata.

Misurata, a few miles inland, had a main street, and what looked like a place for an open air market down the centre. We saw the usual cream coloured buildings, a Friday mosque with its slender minaret, and small groups of Arab men standing around here and there. It all seemed very hot and dusty. Misurata Marina, no longer important by the 20th century, lay about 7 miles away to the east and had been in its day an important port for Thubactis, as the Romans called Misurata. We, however, had arrived in the town centre itself, still an important market and, as a town in Tripolitania, second only to Tripoli itself.

'I could do with a long cold drink. Where's that hotel?'

Misurata. Market day in the 1950s.

We found the small detached Italianate Hotel Misurata; it felt cool and dark inside. A middle-aged Italian lady dressed in black greeted us, showed us our room, and explained about meals speaking in Italian with the occasional English word, so that somehow or other we managed to understand. That evening, we devoured an absolutely delicious spaghetti bolognese and some water and wine, and settled into our Misurata holiday.

A small sitting room had a gramophone and a few 78 rpm records. The one that attracted us however, and the only one I now remember from that holiday, was Edith Piaf singing, *La Vie en Rose*.

'Do you hear that?' said Dave, '"Mon coeur qui bat". Know what it means?'

'Yes' I said, 'My heart which beats.'

'My beating heart!' he replied. 'My heart missed a few beats when I got those call-up papers: do you remember all that?' I certainly did remember.

'Yes, and it certainly raced quite a bit during all that basic training: doesn't it all seem a long time ago now? I wonder how Dave Jeeves and all the others are getting on. He went to Germany didn't he? D'you remember? And, Alan Kirkwood, and John Jordan, and Jim Gibbons, and Peter Crawshaw – "Foulmouth"! A very unfair name *you* gave him!'

'Yes! And don't forget Hudson! Meanwhile, back at that ranch!'

'Of course! And that trip to Wigan, and Wigan Pier!'

We chatted about our service and the old times, and I put him in the picture about 6RTR and the Homs that he knew so well, while he rekindled for me some fond memories of Tripoli and Piccola Capri, describing his exploits in that lovely city and how he felt about 68AEC.

We enjoyed a lazy holiday wandering around Misurata, eating well in the hotel and making friends with some Italian friars who, we discovered, had a house in the town. We had noticed them, in their familiar brown habits, and they had invited us in for some refreshment. They spoke no English but they were able nevertheless to invite us for a game of 'bocce', a game of bowls played on the hard sandy ground. We played it most days amid gales of laughter, and, though we never reached the degree of skill of our hosts, they let us win occasionally.

After a couple of days in the intense inland heat, we decided to find the sea, and cool off with a swim. With a few vague directions in Italian from the lady in the hotel, and a rough idea that the sea lay a few miles to the north of us, we set off down a likely looking track. We set off optimistically but, considering that we had been in North Africa for two summers, we were very foolish and remiss in taking no water with us. Soon we felt quite exhausted, and stopped from time to time to rest under a tree. We seemed to walk miles, and indeed we did, for the sea lay quite a bit further from the town than we had anticipated. But we had no intention of turning back, and eventually we found ahead of us, the blue Mediterranean.

We wandered along the totally deserted beach. Then we enjoyed a magnificent swim and cooled off. We dozed in the sun for a while, but felt both hungry and thirsty by this time, and faced a considerable walk back to Misurata. We cursed our folly in not bringing water and food.

At that moment, we heard a shout and over on some rocks, we spotted an Arab family: a couple of adults, and a few children. We noticed that the woman was not totally covered like the Arabs of Tripoli or Homs. The man beckoned us to come over. We moved across, a bit hesitantly. We were not used to Arabs being all that friendly, except those who worked for the Army. They had a fire going, with a huge pot of some sort of stew cooking and it smelt very inviting. They spoke no English, but he indicated that we could share the meal, which they were all eating out of the common pot, using fingers. All our instincts and army training told us that we should not eat such food (in Tripoli and Homs we could only eat in a place that had been officially approved). But we felt so tired and hungry and the people acted so hospitably, that we succumbed, and enjoyed a delicious Arab supper.

We expressed our thanks in sign language, but still felt very thirsty and made signs to that effect, though they seemed to have nothing at all to drink. Our host, however indicated that he had understood us and began to dig ferociously with his hands into the sand. The hole got deeper and deeper, and eventually to our amazement we saw water. He continued digging until quite a pool of water lay at the bottom. He scooped up some in a small bowl and offered it to us to drink saying in English, 'Sweet, sweet.'

We were so thirsty, and thinking of the long walk back to Misurata, and thinking too that we could not hurt his feelings after he had been so good to us, we decided to drink it. It tasted cool and delicious and we completely quenched our thirst. Then after saying our good-byes and giving our thanks profusely in sign language, we set off for the long trek back.

'We'll be lucky not to get the trots after eating that food,' I remarked

'And drinking that water!' added Dave.

'But it'll be worth it. It saved our lives!'

After an hour or so our steps slowed, and we saw no sign of Misurata.

'Are we on the right road?'

'Let's have a sit down and think about it. It'll get dark soon, and then we'll be for it!' We felt very tired and I could easily have stretched out there and then and closed my eyes.

At that moment, out from behind a rock, emerged an Arab boy of about twelve. He came up and speaking in Arabic began to gesture urgently to us to follow him. Dave and I looked at each other, nodded to each other, and set off. Five minutes later we found ourselves in a group of small Arab dwellings, and the boy led us into one of them. A tall man came towards us speaking in English.

He explained that his boy had spotted us and had returned to tell his father. The father, sensing we might be lost and tired, had sent him out again to fetch us back. It was not far to Misurata, he explained, and after having some tea and bread he would instruct his son to guide us back by the easiest route. He explained that he had worked with the British Army during the war and liked the British people. He wanted to learn about us and our homes and was intrigued by the differences between my England and Dave's Scotland. He was a charming man whom I remember with affection. We exchanged, I recall, addresses which we wrote on cigarette packets, before starting back. We had met our second helpful and welcoming family in the Misurata area. Someone had said once that the Arabs in the more eastern parts of Libya were more friendly than those in the west. They certainly proved friendly on that particular day when we really did need friendship and I shall always be grateful to them.

We stayed a few more days, and had a few more games of bocce. We enjoyed ourselves and suffered no after effects from the eating and drinking on the beach: perhaps we had just become immune. Eventually the time came to board that Arab bus again, and return to Homs, where Dave spent the night, renewing old friendships in the mess before he got a lift back to Tripoli.

* * *

Alain had a girlfriend, Lorna, the daughter of a civil engineer attached to the Army in Tripoli. Alain played rugger superbly, and his rugby playing for the regiment got him into Tripoli more often than would otherwise have been the case, and so he had met the girl of his dreams. He married her shortly after national service ended and invited me to the wedding.

Lorna had a lovely red open-topped Triumph TR2 which he sometimes used to borrow to ease the transport problems of getting up and down between Tripoli and Homs at weekends. This added another dimension to my life because when he had the TR2 at Homs for the week it became useful transport for both of us, and we could get out for the occasional trip into the desert. Indeed sometimes we took a .22 rifle and enjoyed a bit of shooting. Alain taught me to drive, and so I did a bit of driving too, enjoying the car's fantastic acceleration. When I subsequently took my test in UK and started driving normal cars I could not believe how sluggish they all seemed. Once he invited me go down to Tripoli with him for the weekend and I stayed over at Lorna's grand house by the sea, for a big house party: it may have been their engagement party, I cannot now remember, but I do remember my pleasure in revisiting even briefly my old haunts.

The TR2 was not the only thing that Alain brought from his trips to Tripoli. One day he arrived clutching a box containing a Siamese cat called Henry, a present from Lorna. We set Henry free in our room, and he began prancing around in a very lordly and aristocratic manner. Alain had brought a silver dish in which he had been instructed to place the cat's food. Such a grand cat could not eat out of an ordinary dish. Henry impressed us, with his blue eyes, greyish-blue smooth coat and very aloof bearing. He appeared not to approve of us mere sergeants. Perhaps he would have been more at home in the officers' mess. We dared not let him out of the room till he had settled, but we provided a dish of water, and a litter-tray, and our lance corporal brought in the best food available from the mess kitchen. We became quite fond of our new companion.

After only a few days however, we returned from an afternoon on the beach to find our beloved cat missing. Our fine wire mesh covering our open window had one small hole, incredibly torn out by the cat. He had escaped! We ran out and searched everywhere. Henry was nowhere to be found. We put a notice in the regimental newspaper asking for any information on the cat's whereabouts: all to no avail.

Alain, distraught, said we must not let Lorna know that we had lost her cat!

Several days later, as we strolled in the village, a great colony of the Homs wild cats raced past, and there, in the lead, pirouetted Henry, our Siamese! He had taken over leadership of the pack, as befitted such a superior and highly intelligent creature.

Alain and I looked at each other and knew that we would never get him back now, which perhaps was just as well.

Alain had his girl-friend to occupy his dreams. I had the *Homs Weekly Gazette* to give me the occasional nightmare. Early on I had been told that I had inherited the job of editing the *Gazette*, our weekly regimental newspaper, I looked through some past copies to gain some idea of its flavour. It consisted of gossipy news about the camp, a few jokes, a crossword, letters to the editor, some items of serious news and bits of army news. Fortunately we had some regular reporters scattered around the barrack rooms and in the corporals' mess and I just had to go on my rounds and collect the news. I also had my crossword compiler. The education centre received regular hard news from army news sources which could always be used to fill up space. I would get it all together, edit it as necessary, and then take it up to the orderly room, where Sergeant Steer and his clerks would get to work typing it out. Then it circulated around the barracks and was I think much appreciated. I found editing interesting not least because it got me around the barrack rooms and elsewhere, meeting people, and collecting articles and news ready for the weekly issue.

It has to be said however, that the orderly room typing was not all that it should have been, and typing errors, and some eccentric spelling did creep into the paper, which led to some amused comment in various quarters.

After a few weeks of successful publishing, and continued typing and spelling errors, I received a letter from a senior officer, a major, who clearly possessed a nice sense of humour.

He was not a squadron commander but had another position connected with leisure activities, the PRI (President of the Regimental Institute).

Dear Sir,
I would like to say how much I enjoy reading the articles in the Weekly Gazette.
They are invariably entertaining and informative. However, a fow errors do crep in from to tim and this dos botther me sligtly.
Perhapps in wood helpp if occansioll y someon mude on atempt to chuck thh spelint und t
bfoooo ittt a;;s??&** s00 + neegyyytakkajebc7 doo09 qqqrradszzvzhiititpp-++
oofgfhyooooldleocooooooooohhh!! Wwwwwiiiiiirrrrrroooo./. Yr77rts llllllllllllllllllll00?""%9

David Horton (Major)

I thought it a pretty funny letter, and I determined to put it in the next issue. The orderly room to their credit typed it, and it duly appeared in print. A number of people congratulated me on it. I wondered if there would be any follow-up letters.

I had not reckoned with the view of the adjutant however. The adjutant, a captain, and a key figure in any regiment, was among other things in charge of discipline and the orderly room. Though a man of many qualities, possessing a sense of humour seemed not to be one of them!

I received a message summoning me to the adjutant's office at 10.30 a.m. I went up the stairs in the admin. block wondering what on earth it could be about. They told me to wait because Major Horton was in there with him. Major Horton? Could it possibly be about the letter? Would the adjutant congratulate us?

I waited a good ten minutes and I could hear raised voices. Eventually the door opened, and the major left looking extremely subdued and very tight-lipped; the adjutant barked at me, 'Come in!'

I went in, and saluted. He seemed quite put out and made no attempt to hide it. He came straight to the point. He did not like the letter which insulted his clerks in the orderly room who did a damned fine job. He was not prepared to tolerate it and he wanted to know what I meant by choosing to publish it.

'Well, sir, I thought it was a very funny letter and ...'

Captain Weaving however was not in the mood to listen to excuses. It was not in the least funny as far as the typists were concerned, men who worked very hard and conscientiously and ...'

'I appreciate your point, sir, but I didn't intend ...'

The adjutant however was not concerned with what I intended, but only with the effects that it might have on morale. My job at the *Gazette* was to raise morale, not to destroy it. I should have known better ...

'Well, sir, a senior officer sent it in and ...'

Captain Weaving refused to be impressed by that excuse either and he reminded me that I, as editor, was responsible for its publication.

'Yes, sir, I am sorry that it may have had adverse effects. I shall take more care in the future.'

The adjutant ended the interview with a curt nod.

I came to attention, saluted, turned about, and left.

I felt not in the least put out by this episode. The letter had been a good one, and an appropriate response would have been for someone to send a reply, preferably an amusing one, and then the matter would have been closed. Nevertheless I knew that the rules dictated that I should just accept the adjutant's rebuke and then get on with my job.

However the episode did point to an interesting side of army life. I now knew that the adjutant would stand up for his men, and his department. They were like that in RTR, loyal to each other. It is probably unfair to accuse him of lacking a sense of humour. He just did not find it funny when a senior officer appeared to be enjoying a joke at the expense of the regimental clerks. If the joke had been against himself, I dare say he would have taken it in good part.

I also noticed that other things than rank mattered in the Army: position counted far more. The adjutant, a captain, held a lower rank than the major who wrote the letter, but he held a far more important position, and had clearly rebuked the major severely before calling me in. Again, though merely a sergeant, in my position as editor I could have, and should have according to the adjutant, rejected the major's letter.

Likewise, Major Green, our boss at the education centre, had the same rank as half a dozen majors in the regiment, but as second-in-command of the regiment, he outranked them all. The orderly sergeant, when wearing his sash of office, had enormous powers which took him to a position well above that of his normal rank of sergeant.

I carried on editing the weekly paper, but I now carefully scrutinised everything before submitting it to the orderly room. It would not do to be up before the adjutant again!

And, it must be said, the quality of the orderly room typing did improve no end, after that incident of the letter! So the point had been successfully made.

* * *

The Homs summer continued with our happy routine of morning parades, orderly sergeant duties, work in the morning with Mac who had fully recovered, afternoons on the beach, and evenings in the mess. I took occasional visitors to Leptis and continued to edit the newspaper. Alain paid weekend visits to his fiancée in Tripoli. Prinn and indeed Azizia already seemed distant to me. Meanwhile various squadrons occasionally left the barracks to go on military exercises and on one memorable day helicopters dropped from the sky onto the square when the Royal Marine Commandos 'attacked' Homs. It took me back to the 'attack' we had suffered at Beaconsfield. I now felt totally part of 6RTR and enjoyed my life at Homs: something very different from life at Azizia, more military, more regimental. Life in Tripoli had been fun, and I missed old friends, but my transfer had certainly widened my experience, and I had no regrets. Indeed if there had been any moves at that point to transfer me back to Tripoli, I should have felt quite miserable about it.

Homs. Tankies outside their squadron block.

In that late summer, a notice went up emphasising again the military side of Homs life. It concerned training in the use of the Stirling sub-machine gun, introduced to replace the sten. The orderly room had posted a list of sergeants, including me, and the names of troopers whom we must supervise on the range in the use of the weapon. Somehow, they assumed that we would all be skilled in the use of the Stirling and could instruct others in its use! I had scarcely handled a weapon since leaving the UK but 6RTR expected all sergeants to be experts in all matters military so I should not have been surprised at the notice.

Fortunately, the sergeant in charge of the armoury seemed to know all about it. I asked him to show me how it worked and I practised firing it at the cut-out targets. Essentially I found it a superior and more accurate sten gun and not too difficult to master. The East Lancs had given us all good training in weapon use. When their turn came, the troopers seemed surprisingly good and mastered the Stirling without difficulty. The episode took me back to basic training at a time when my military service was drawing to a close: a last fling before the whole experience ended.

I found those final weeks strange. Alain and I often discussed it, just as I had discussed it before on the beach in Tripoli. We seemed to have been in the Army forever, and to have lived abroad forever. Parades, uniforms, army acronyms and work as an army instructor seemed a permanent part of life. Those days when we had been naïve university students, thinking ourselves so clever, and actually thinking we had been working hard, seemed a lifetime away, as did that day of graduation dressed in gown and hood. Army service had appeared as a completely odd form of life when I embarked upon it at Fulwood Barracks, Preston, almost two years earlier; now it had become reality and normality. I knew I had to return to civilian life in a couple of months but I viewed the prospect with a sense of bewilderment and a little apprehension, and, yes, sadness too, rather than joy. All this RTR life and all that I had learnt and adapted to so painfully at times, and all these friends with whom I had lived so closely, would be snatched away forever. Because we understood that, I think we became aware of needing to have a last long walk along the beach, a last meal at Zacchi's, a last look at Leptis. We almost savoured those last parades, and lessons, and evenings in the mess. And it helped that the whole regiment was preparing to leave too.

My sense of total detachment from my old student life came vividly into focus with the arrival of visitors to Homs in the late summer, post-graduate geography students, apparently doing some sort of research for some sort of 'higher' degree. They had requested that the Army in Libya put them up and we did so for a couple of weeks. They lounged about, shameless with their longish floppy hair, laid-back, languid, and calculatedly casual. I suspected that they thought us soldiers a bit odd, sounding reveille, lowering the flag, wearing well starched and creased KD, saluting, and mucking about with tanks and guns and scout cars! I knew university students only too well! But I had moved on and now felt only contempt for their feigned superiority and arrogance. I hated the very sight of them! I refused to speak to them or have anything to do with them. I totally despised them and what I considered to be their pointless and ridiculous research.

'They're doing this so-called research just to avoid national service,' I remarked to Alain, who had the exact same view as I had. Fortunately they did not stay long.

About mid-August Alain Bain left for Tripoli and his flight home. 'Look out for the wedding invitation. See you then,' he shouted as he was driven out through the gate. I missed him. We had become close friends, just as I had been with that other room-mate, Alan Goodson.

6RTR never replaced Alain. The whole regiment busily prepared to return home to Britain. It would take 16 days, calling in at Cyprus, Malta, and Gibraltar. I heard that as we would arrive in Southampton just before my demob date in September, I would sail back with them.

* * *

9

Too quickly, too sharply, and too soon

Dunera looked elegant and still as she lay there in Tripoli harbour. The scene around her however buzzed with relentless activity. Everybody seemed purposeful, moving slowly but determinedly about his business. Rows of young troopers, dressed in their tropical KD, boarded the ship, walking steadily up the long gangplank. I saw women too, army wives, and their children who had been at the Tripoli army school. Trucks that had transported us all down from Homs to Tripoli seemed to be parked all over the place in the square. I thought of the old song sung in the mess at Azizia: the one about the troopship just leaving Bombay, 'bound for old Blighty's shore.' The song had come to life; a whole regiment was leaving. After long service overseas, including action at Suez, it was returning to Blighty: an evocative sight.

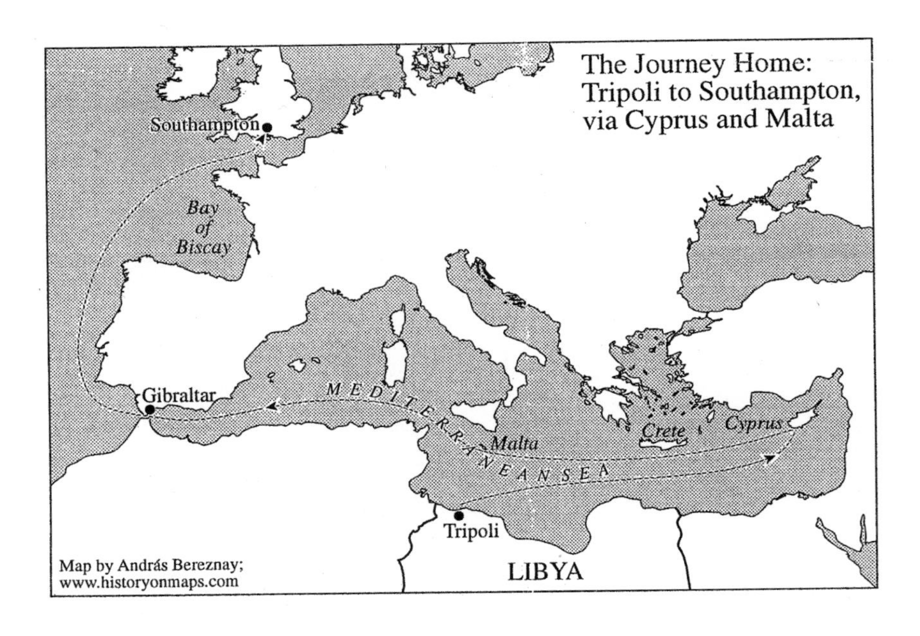

I recognised the place of course, the castle, and the old city. I saw the familiar streets radiating off, and I brought to mind the first time we had alighted from a gharry on our first visit to that square. I thought of all those subsequent visits and above all I felt again the almost tangible atmosphere of that city, so different from the atmosphere at Homs. This had been my city for such a long time, a city I had become fond of. I was so glad to be leaving this way, by ship: a slow way with time to think and mentally say goodbye to Libya, Tripoli, and indeed a whole way of life. To have been whisked away from Idris Airport by plane would have been too sudden, too final. I needed to sail away gently through the blue Mediterranean, taking every one of the sixteen days we had been told it would take, so that Tripoli and Homs could, like old soldiers, just fade away.

As I made my way aboard my eyes roamed everywhere. I had never been on the water before other than rowing a boat in the park at home, or on that trip we once took down the river on a small pleasure craft. *Dunera* may not have been a huge liner, but it certainly impressed me. As I wandered along the deck trying to work out how to get to the sergeants' section and find my quarters, I heard the tremendous roar of a sergeant major in full flow. There he stood: the ship's RSM, a towering figure with an enormous bristling moustache. Letting fly at some of our troopers, he showed in unmistakable terms that for them this would be no pleasure cruise. As I approached he glared at me in hostile fashion, and for a second I felt like a recruit in basic training about to be reduced to shreds by this intimidating monster. However my three tapes must have stopped him in his tracks for he turned away to scream at an unfortunate young trooper approaching from another direction.

The warrant officers and staff sergeants had, unusually, been separated from the sergeants. They had their own shared cabins and dining-room, and as things turned out, we hardly ever saw them. We had our own large common area aft, with slung hammock-beds, which I found comfortable enough. We had our own ablutions and our own dining-room, fairly small, as there were only some fifteen of us. Rather ominously, the table had a ridge round its outside to stop dishes rolling off in rough weather.

I went on deck to watch the ship cast off. As *Dunera* pulled slowly away I caught a new view of Tripoli, with its domes and minarets and palm trees, and the city looked dazzlingly white and more beautiful than ever. Land drifted slowly farther away, till it eventually became just a smudge on the horizon, and vanished.

We sailed eastwards, heading for Limassol in Cyprus, in order to pick up troops from another regiment. So we had embarked on a real Mediterranean cruise, from Tripoli which lay roughly in the centre, to the far eastern end where Cyprus lay, back past Crete to Malta, then westwards to Gibraltar.

I eventually went down to the dining-room for our early evening meal. A kilted Black Watch soldier, a young national serviceman from Alloa, served us dinner. He came with the ship I think and would be looking after us sergeants on board.

Everyone seemed to have a job of sorts on the ship: the troopers had to be kept busy with fatigues and training, though always remaining wary of the ship's RSM who kept a tight grip, working of course with the RTR officers and NCOs. They gave me a job that I certainly did not expect. I had to devise an educational programme for about a dozen children on board, aged from about 7 to 16. They provided us with a pleasant room leading straight from the deck, with large windows and excellent views, and plenty of paper and writing materials, and told me to get on with it. Later in its life *Dunera* became an educational cruise ship, and I like to think that I was an original pioneer of that rôle as I received my baptism on that voyage into teaching children, a very different experience I might say from teaching young national service soldiers.

I decided to teach them about *Dunera*, the Royal Tanks, and the Mediterranean Sea, its geography and history, and bring in English and mathematics where relevant. So I rapidly mapped out a course covering the Ancient Egyptians and their Pyramids, the Holy Land, the Crusades, Cyprus and recent troubles, Greece and its fascinating history, Rome and its empire, and Malta and its courage during World War II, and Gibraltar, and the Mediterranean climate. Then I set to work. I remember them as good, well behaved and well motivated children and the scheme worked successfully: the voyage after all fascinated them just as it fascinated me and of course we worked mornings only.

In spite of the best efforts of the ship's RSM to make everybody's life a misery the trip became very enjoyable. We found it pleasantly warm: it was still late August. And the sea remained calm on the way to Cyprus. We enjoyed good food and the young Scot looked after us well. We could all have a drink and socialise in the evening.

After a few days we approached Limassol in Cyprus. Here more soldiers joined us. Limassol, with its typical low Mediterranean white and creamy buildings, looked peaceful and serene in the hot sun, masking for the moment the misery and resentment and violence that lay just under the surface on that beautiful island. Nobody was allowed ashore.

After a few hours, we put to sea again, this time heading westward, and Cyprus slipped back over the horizon. The first couple of hours passed peacefully enough but soon the smooth gentle cruise that we had been enjoying for some days gave way to something a little different. The swell on the sea became noticeably heavier. *Dunera* began to rock slowly fore and aft, dipping her bow into the sea which then splashed and sprayed onto the foredeck as the ship rose sharply out of the water. People had to hold onto anything to hand as they went about their business. Within another hour the ship rocked slowly but by then severely. I stood on deck and watched the stern rise and rise for what seemed like a full minute till the deck was sharply angled and walking became all but impossible. At the same time the whole Mediterranean Sea seemed to crash over the bows, soaking everything within reach. The stern then fell and fell, as if it would never stop falling. With the deck at last level again, it would continue to dip and dip, while the bow rose higher and higher into the air till standing again became impossible and people had to cling to anything within reach. All this seemed to be in slow motion. The sea did not look particularly rough though I noticed the worsening swell. In my teaching area the furniture slid all over the place, and the youngsters stumbled and slipped and crawled around helplessly. Most ended up sitting as best they could on the floor. Work became impossible. Out on deck a number of very young children (under five) appeared to have been placed in a sort of cage where they sat crying and being sick.

After completing the morning's work, I made my way below for lunch. I could see the familiar faces of many troopers sitting on the stairs, moaning, and generally looking miserable. The young Scot who served our food tried his best but could scarcely cross the floor and started slipping and sliding his way to the table. On the table itself food and glasses and plates went crashing down to one end and then the other: had it not been for the useful ridge round the table's edge everything would have ended up on the floor. Everyone took it in good part and those who actually felt up to it laughed aloud at our ridiculous predicament. No one wanted much food anyway. I certainly felt decidedly below par. And we had no escape: that night our hammock-beds swung around quite violently and I fell asleep feeling that my whole being was in perpetual motion.

The following day showed no improvement. The ship seemed to be in permanent slow rocking mode, the deck moving constantly between a 45° slope one way, and then the other. Walking around required the sort of sea legs most of us had yet to develop. However, in true military fashion, everyone carried on with work. Many people became seasick: the children especially so. Only the redoubtable RSM appeared perfectly normal. This crazy state of affairs continued for about four days, and became our way of life. Like most people, I had no appetite, and in any case nothing stayed still on the table for more than a few seconds. In my ignorance I had thought the Mediterranean a calm sea. If the Mediterranean could behave like this, I pondered, what would the Bay of Biscay be like – or the Atlantic Ocean? Flying out had been rough for an hour or two and I recalled our failure to land at Nice, but sailing could be sheer misery for days on end. How I pitied those national servicemen in the Royal Navy.

As we approached Malta however things began to calm down. The sun shone gloriously, and we prepared, after several days at sea, for a relaxing spell on dry land. Valletta looked just as majestic as I had remembered it, though now much warmer, in late summer sun. A burnished creamy-brown was the prevailing colour. Grand Harbour particularly impressed me when approached from the sea, and I saw numerous ships, including a sleek cruise liner. Elderly passengers wandered around her decks and I wondered if they, poor things, had just come through what we had come through. I vowed then that in years to come nothing would ever persuade me to go on a Mediterranean cruise!

I looked forward to going ashore and renewing my acquaintance with Valletta, and my mind returned to that night we spent there on the way out in winter, a year and a half earlier. I thought of those who had flown out with me, Dave and Lawrence whom I had known since Fulwood, and the others who had been with me at Beaconsfield. Were they still in Tripoli, preparing to fly out to UK? Would they too call in again at Malta? *Dunera* would dock in Southampton on 9 September, and they would probably fly out on or about the same day. For a moment, as I stood there, I really missed them, and wished them there with me on the ship. I visualised Alain Bain in Galashiels, preparing to get on with his life and looking forward to his wedding. And where was that old horse Alan Goodson? Demobbed by now, of course.

One or two of us went ashore together, including Jock, the Scots lad from Alloa who worked in our mess and whom I persuaded, with some difficulty, not to go looking for a girl down the Gut, but rather to have a look around Valletta. We went out to see the famous church at Mosta. Malta had had a tough time during the war, and a bomb had fallen right through the church's great dome. Luckily, or miraculously, depending upon your point of view, the bomb had not exploded and damage had been minimal.

Back on *Dunera,* we enjoyed a good meal in a dining-room no longer lurching about like a mad thing. We set sail for Gibraltar and spent the next few days in glorious hot sun and calm seas. We also had the company of a bewildered elderly couple who, unbelievably, belonged to the cruise liner in Valletta Harbour but had somehow managed to board the wrong ship. We certainly relished our food for a change and of course we took the chance of a drink in the evening and walks around the deck. Perhaps Mediterranean cruising was not so bad after all.

Then Gibraltar swung into sight, and we explored ashore again. I found Gibraltar quite remarkable with its apes and its great rock but it felt curiously English in its atmosphere, and I began to feel my Mediterranean and North African experience disappearing As we sailed out into the Atlantic we discarded for the last time our KD shorts and tunics, and donned BD once again. Somehow the change seemed symbolic: a long dream was coming to an end as we headed north into the Bay of Biscay.

After a beautifully calm voyage through the Bay we sighted the shores of England and soon after we docked at Southampton in lovely warm weather: 1959 had been one of the best summers on record. We had returned home at last, after what seemed years and years of absence.

Going ashore involved once again all that slow-motion activity, the lines of people, all the baggage. I had to collect my Army Book 111 (Certificate of National Service) with its hand-written testimonial signed by the CO. I grabbed my kit-bag and moved off.

I said goodbye to all those people that I had come to know so well and goodbye to a whole way of life. The final moment had come as it always does, too quickly, too sharply, and too soon, and I found myself standing alone on that platform in Southampton, thinking of my journey to London and Beaconsfield, as 6RTR boarded the train taking them home to their depôt in Dorset.

My journey to London passed uneventfully and once again I found myself at Marylebone. The little train to Beaconsfield had not changed in a year and a half: I doubt if it had changed in a hundred years! Before long we puffed into Seer Green station which looked delightful in the warm summer weather. I did not seem to remember all the trees, but then I had seen the place before only in that cold bare winter. And there in front of me stood the familiar little bridge which I crossed to the parking area, and the road to Beaconsfield.

I found a telephone and rang Wilton Park Camp.

'Sergeant Kelly here. Due for demob at the end of national service. Will you send some transport please?'

I found the dark green Land Rover difficult to place after those sandy coloured vehicles in Homs and Tripoli. I said little to the driver: I could not identify with him either. My people had gone off to Bovington: this boy was a stranger who had probably never served abroad. What did he know about anything? The Buckinghamshire countryside looked lush and stunning on that glorious summer's day, but I had already begun to miss the sand and dust of Tripoli and Homs. Would I ever see them again? And even if I did, I could never feel the same without all the friends I had known there. I knew deep down that I had to move on but I still had a feeling almost of bereavement.

The camp looked familiar (depressingly so) and I saw some recruit-instructors in training, just as my intake had been in training a lifetime ago, but I felt a stranger there, knowing nobody. Mechanically I dealt with the formalities of handing-in kit, carefully removing as keepsakes the red/gold shoulder flashes of 6RTR. I received my final travel warrant and three weeks terminal leave, and left.

Back in Seer Green station, with my kit-bag and all the bits and pieces that the Army did not want, I waited for the London train, alone with my thoughts.

The train for Marylebone arrived at last and, as I sat there in the little compartment, eyes closed, I heard once again that familiar voice: 'Seer Green, Seer Green, calling at Gerrards Cross, Denham …'

I lay back, almost in a trance as other voices and images began to enter my subconscious. Could that be Corporal Bowerbank? 'Swing those arms back! Left, right! Left right!' And there next to him Sergeant Griffiths, complete with red sash, and just behind him CSM Stott of the Irish Guards? They all seemed to be at Azizia Barracks in Tripoli. And surely that must be Nobby Norman standing on the square at Homs shouting out 'Fetch Sergeant Bain.' In the far distance I could just make out countless young lads laughing on the beach and running down towards the sea seemingly without a care in the world.

Then, as the images faded I saw again, in my mind's eye, those hands slowly waving out of the window as that train bearing away the 6th Royal Tanks rounded the bend and disappeared out of sight.

It was all over.

THE END

CERTIFICATE OF DISCHARGE (*To be retained by the soldier*)

Page 2
Army
Book
111

Having completed whole-time service under the National Service Acts, 1948 to 1950, you are liable to further part-time service in the AER/TA unit to which you are posted until you have completed a total of five and a half years' service in all.

If this certificate is lost or mislaid no duplicate can be obtained.

Any unauthorized alterations of the particulars in this certificate may render the holder liable to prosecution under the Seamen's and Soldiers' False Characters Act, 1906.

ARMY NO. 23418269 RANK SGT

SURNAME (Block Capitals) KELLY

CHRISTIAN OR FORE NAME(S) (Block Capitals) JOHN

UNIT, REGT. OF CORPS

for which enlisted RAEC

from which discharged RAEC

Service began on 12·9·57 at PRESTON

Effective date of discharge from wholetime service 11·9·59

Total amount of full-time reckonable service 2 YR

Reason for discharge NS RELEASE

Description of Soldier on Completion of Whole-time Service

Date of birth 23·12·35 Height 5 ft. 8 1/2 ins.

Complexion FRESH Eyes BLUE Hair BROWN

Marks and Scars (visible) VAC SCAR L. ARM

Trade Qualifications

CIVILIAN TRADE STUDENT

SERVICE TRADE EDN. INSTRUCTOR

FINAL EMPLOYMENT EDN. INSTRUCTOR

Courses and Tests passed